Writing from Life

BOOKS BY HEATHER ROBERTSON

NON-FICTION

Reservations Are for Indians (1970)
Grass Roots (1973)
Salt of the Earth (1974)
A Terrible Beauty: The Art of Canada at War (1977)
The Flying Bandit (1981)
*More Than a Rose: Prime Ministers, Wives and
Other Women* (1991)
On the Hill: A People's Guide to Canada's Parliament (1992)
*Driving Force: The McLaughlin Family and
the Age of the Car* (1995)

FICTION

Willie: A Romance (1983)
Lily: A Rhapsody in Red (1986)
Igor: A Novel of Intrigue (1989)

ANTHOLOGIES

Her Own Woman (1975)
Canada's Newspapers: The Inside Story (1980)
From the Country (1991)

Writing from Life

A Guide to Writing True Stories

HEATHER ROBERTSON

M&S

Canadian Cataloguing in Publication Data

Robertson, Heather, 1942 –
Writing from life : a guide for writing true stories

Includes bibliographical references.
ISBN 0-7710-7558-8

1. Exposition (Rhetoric).   I. Title.

PN187.R62   1998   808'.042   C98-930122-2

We acknowledge the financial support of the Government of Canada through the Book Publishing Industry Development Program for our publishing activities. We further acknowledge the support of the Canada Council for the Arts and the Ontario Arts Council for our publishing program.

Typeset in Minion by M&S, Toronto
Printed and bound in Canada

McClelland & Stewart Inc.
The Canadian Publishers
481 University Avenue
Toronto, Ontario
M5G 2E9

1 2 3 4 5   02 01 00 99 98

Pages 219-22 constitute a continuation of the copyright page.

Contents

Introduction

Writing from Life has grown out of my thirty-five years as a professional writer, first as a student, then as a newspaper reporter, columnist, magazine writer, and author of books of documentary, fiction, social history, and biography. For more than twenty-five years I have been self-employed. I work hard to make an unpredictable, often precarious living, but I am able to choose my projects and set my own timetable. I get tired and discouraged at times, and wished I'd studied law, but I have no regrets. I didn't choose to be a journalist, journalism chose me. When I was a little girl in Winnipeg, CBC Radio ran a series of short stories about the adventures of another little girl, named Maggie Muggins. Maggie Muggins became my friend, and every day she signed off cheerily, saying, "I don't know what will happen tomorrow!" Good advice, Maggie, I thought, and followed it.

This book reflects my own background, tastes, and prejudices. It is a guide, not a formula. As examples, I have chosen writers' work that illustrates the points I am trying to make and publications that are reasonably available in bookstores and libraries. Some of these stories have won prizes, others have not.

My choices are arbitrary. These writers are not necessarily better than others. I omit many writers whose stories I admire, and no doubt I will omit writers you admire. Some I omit because I don't like their work, others because their stories have become dated or embarrassing. American storyteller Sherwood Anderson, for instance, writes about "niggers" as he would dogs or horses, and George Orwell's depictions of "the Jew" in his early book, *Down and Out in Paris and London* (Gollancz, 1933), are repugnant. Orwell also disguises identities, including his own (his real name was Eric Blair), fabricates events, and suppresses significant information (his well-to-do English parents would not have let him starve). Don't follow the fashions of political correctness, but if you want to offend someone, know who and why.

I have tried to choose examples that don't require privileged access. Most political stories, for instance, are written by professional staff reporters fortunate enough to be on the spot at the right time, or who, like Carl Bernstein and Bob Woodward of Watergate fame, are able to spend years cultivating their sources. Their success is often more a matter of timing and contacts than literary skill.

I give short shrift to humour writing. Events are often funny in themselves and many are rich with satiric possibilities. Every writer should take advantage of these opportunities. But I am impatient with writers who wink at their readers, laugh at their own jokes, or inflate banal situations to cartoon proportions. If you feel you have a talent for comedy, write for television, movies, or the stage. You'll make more money.

I also ignore writing that has a vocabulary and formula all its own, a code almost unintelligible to outsiders. These literary subcultures include sports commentary, scholarly articles, government documents, and corporate publications, although the success of business books such as *The Wealthy Barber* (David Chilton, Stoddart, 1989) has helped to break down the "bullshit baffles brains" mystique of corpspeak. Some scholars do break the academic mould.

I didn't realize it until I had finished the first draft of my manuscript, but my selections reflect the fact that we define news as bad news. Journalism's literary roots reach back to war, espionage, and political strife, and in many countries, journalists are still imprisoned, tortured, and murdered. The Fourth Estate of the British parliament came into being to provide reporters with some protection against kidnapping and assassination by outraged kings and politicians. The advice I give in this book assumes a society where free speech is respected and upheld in law.

Young reporters start out writing obituaries, then graduate to the crime-and-accident beat, a rough rite of passage that includes visiting victims' families to get a quote and a photograph of the deceased. Murder trials are fodder for the front page, and foreign stories usually involve violence, pestilence, or famine. Bad news contains all the ingredients of good stories; good news is no news.

I have two purposes in writing this book. The first is to establish the journal, and journalism, as a legitimate, mainstream literary form. All literature is creative, and when people rise up to defend freedom of speech these days, they are usually defending journalism.

My second purpose is to offer a resource to writers who may not define themselves as journalists, novelists, or short story writers. Literary definitions are becoming blurred, and the electronic age will blur them further. Anyone can produce a manuscript. Who will read it? How good is it?

I am assuming that aspiring writers know how to spell, use words with more than two syllables, and construct paragraphs out of sentences (this is more difficult than you may think). This book is not a style guide. Plenty of style guides are available in libraries and bookstores. If you are a Canadian writer, use a recently pub-lished Canadian guide. Usage changes. For instance, it is no longer acceptable to use "he" as a generic pronoun if "he" also refers to women. To avoid the clumsy "he/she" or "he or she," it is permissi-ble to alternate them or use "they." Better yet, use the plural. Rather than saying "a writer often . . ." say "writers often. . . ."

I have a bias towards writing books. I find the book-length story the most satisfying to write, and, unlike newspaper reporters and magazine journalists, book writers are not constrained by edi-torial policies and editors' prejudices, space, speed, pressure from advertisers, news, trends, and the need to churn out stories about topics that don't interest us.

That said, I learned the basics of story writing on the job at a daily newspaper, and I thrive on the chase and the quick hit. Good books often evolve from newspaper or magazine articles, and as I work on a book, I write magazine stories based on my research. A story is a story, but what exactly *is* a story? That's what this book is about.

CHAPTER 1

Telling the Truth

We all have stories to tell, and secrets to hide. The stories we omit from our life's narrative are as important as the stories we include, the white space between the words as eloquent as the words themselves. Knowing what to tell, and choosing what to leave out, shape a true story as effectively as a make-believe story. When we write about real people, places, and events, we choose a cast of characters, a locale and a plot, and we have the additional constraint of making our narrative conform to the truth.

Discovering the truth, as we shall see, is more difficult for the writer than simply presenting the facts, but if important facts are fudged or concealed, the reader feels cheated. The autobiographies of politicians and celebrities are usually superficial and self-serving, constructed to enhance a public myth created by advertisers, publicists, and the news. The best are written by professional ghost-writers who cast the narrator in a heroic mould, a Prince Valiant or Fairy Queen triumphing over terrible obstacles to achieve fame, fortune, and power. The model they use is John Bunyan's *The Pilgrim's Progress*.

I call this the Mythological School of narrative, and it has dominated the writing of history, biography, and memoir since the heyday of the Victorian Empire. It is based on the assumption that an individual has to be a great leader or a genius, a public figure and a role model, to be worth writing about at all, and the story must instruct and inspire the reader. British essayist Thomas Carlyle popularized this approach in 1841 with *On Heroes, Hero-worship, and the Heroic in History*. Canadian historian Donald Creighton used it with subtlety and effect in his two-volume biography of prime minister Sir John A. Macdonald, Peter C. Newman more bombastically in his three-volume history of the Hudson's Bay Company, and Pierre Berton in his history of the Canadian Pacific Railway. In the United States, Democratic journalists and historians transformed John F. Kennedy into the King of Camelot, and Kennedy established his own mystique in 1956 by writing *Profiles in Courage*.

When history is seen as the narrative of Great Men, publishing an autobiography presents ambitious but obscure men with an opportunity to achieve mythic status. *Iacocca* turned a brash American car manufacturer, Lee Iacocca, into a household name; a Canadian best-seller, *Straight from the Heart*, transformed a "little guy from Shawinigan," Jean Chrétien, into leader of the Liberal Party and later prime minister. Adolf Hitler's political career began with *Mein Kampf*. Hitler's nemesis, British prime minister Sir Winston Churchill, had been a journalist before going into politics, and after the Second World War Churchill wrote his own voluminous history of the events in which he had played a heroic role.

Mythmaking provokes scepticism. I call this the Revisionist or Muckraking School. Recent books have shredded the Kennedy mystique and portrayed his White House as a whorehouse. The debunking approach is popular with women, who have been marginalized in the dominant myth, or omitted altogether. Women are used to washing dirty laundry, and know what an emperor looks like without his clothes.

Mommie Dearest, the monster-mother biography of actress Joan Crawford, written by her daughter, Christina, is the *Iacocca* of revisionism. In Great Britain, Diana, Princess of Wales, demystified the Royal Family, simply by telling her own story. The subsequent avalanche of memoirs, biographies, exposés, and television documentaries by, and about, the Royals, ex-Royals, their friends, lovers, and hangers-on, illustrated how, merely by changing the point of view, a storybook romance could become a tragi-comedy of adultery and deceit. Diana's dramatic death in a car crash spun her story once more into melodrama and myth.

Most narrators are either mythmakers or debunkers. Pierre Berton celebrates "the national dream," Mordecai Richler finds anti-Semites in the nation's attic. Gloria Steinem plays the princess of feminism, Germaine Greer the witch. Norman Mailer shoves his *Advertisements for Myself* in the contemptuous face of satirist Gore Vidal, and their literary feud spins off more memoirs, magazine stories, and television confrontations.

The first question a beginning writer should ask is this: Can I handle criticism? Writing is a public act. Your name is on the story. You can't hide behind a pseudonym (they never work), and because you are telling a true story, you can't fictionalize the events or the people who took part in them (see Chapter 6). Nothing infuriates me more than a story full of nameless people, especially people called only "Mother" and "Father," or discovering that the writer has changed the names of people who are otherwise easily identifiable.

Once your story is on paper, or in your computer database, it demands to be read. Locking up your journal in a drawer only indicates that you expect someone to read it, and encourages them to do so. I often hear people say, "Oh, I'm writing this for myself." My advice is: If your story isn't worth telling, don't write it.

Writing is also a provocative act. A true story involves characters who have their own lives and points of view. They may interpret events differently, or disagree violently with your version. They may be embarrassed, or feel that you have invaded their privacy. For most of us, it's a shock to see our names in print, and we tend to associate this kind of publicity with criminals, politicians, and victims. We all want to appear in a good light, or what we think is a good light, and publishing even the most accurate and innocent story, or showing it to someone involved, may provoke emotional trauma, threats, verbal abuse, or permanent estrangement.

I have experienced all of these responses to my work, most of them unexpected. I have been hanged and burned in effigy. I have been sued for libel. I have been called a Nazi and accused of racism, hysteria, and neurosis. I have made enemies, and lost friends. In my first book, I unwittingly offended my mother, and in a published interview I recorded with broadcaster Barbara Frum, Barbara inadvertently offended her daughter, Linda. Both our relationships weathered the firestorms of tears and recrimination, grief, guilt, and explanation, but we learned the hazards of being too frank about family.

Before you begin to write, ask yourself these questions: Why have I chosen *this* story? What are my motives? Who will read it? Why? Am I confident that my information is complete and accurate? Am I afraid of offending someone? Embarrassing myself? If you have difficulty answering these questions, or the answers make you squeamish, stop and think.

You may have chosen a story you find too frightening or painful to write (see Chapter 6). The solution may be to recast your story as fiction. Fiction allows you freedom to obscure and manipulate, and absolves you of accountability (although not credibility).

Are you able to accept editorial criticism, indifference, or rejection? Will you acknowledge faults and weaknesses in your writing, rewrite and throw out? Having your work evaluated by strangers is a painful and humbling experience. James Lorimer, the publisher of my first book, *Reservations Are for Indians*, cut my huge manuscript in half, then in half again. I could handle that – it was a big improvement – but then I found his editor blithely tossing more of my precious remaining pages into a wastebasket. Furious, I fished them out, and when the editor couldn't explain why he had cut them, I put them back in.

All writers hate criticism. We suffer from anxiety, anger, and depression. We nurse grudges against reviewers, argue fiercely with our editors, and stomp off to find new publishers. This can be therapeutic, and self-destructive.

I long ago adopted the motto: Writers are only as good as our editors. Respecting the editor's advice, however infuriating it may be, helps you distance yourself from your story and see its strengths and flaws. Better to be told in private that your story stinks (editors usually use more diplomatic language, but you get the drift) than be humiliated in print. Criticism should be clear, specific, and constructive: "This is repetitive," or, "How do you know this?" Vague criticism is as useless as vague praise. I once wrote a magazine story for an editor who responded: "I think you should put this through your typewriter again." I did, twice, but my typewriter wasn't clairvoyant, and she eventually rewrote my story, without my permission, to suit herself. That caused a row!

Don't be a literary snob. When I decided at the age of twenty-two to earn my living as a reporter with the *Winnipeg Tribune*, I was warned: "Journalism will ruin your style." What style? How would I develop a style if I didn't write? I recalled that Ernest Hemingway had started with the *Toronto Star*, and Mavis Gallant with the *Montreal Standard*. Charles Dickens had covered the law courts, and like other Victorian novelists, Dickens had published his novels in serial form in the penny press. "No man but a blockhead ever wrote except for money," said the great English man-of-letters Samuel Johnson, and Johnson wrote so well he was rewarded with a royal pension.

Johnson was paid so poorly for his work he *needed* a pension. For every writer who becomes a multi-millionaire, thousands live and die in wretched obscurity. If they are not poor, it's because they have other sources of income: in Canada, freelance writers earn an average of $26,800 a year. Popular taste is fickle, and success depends largely on surfing a wave. The same caution applies to writers who develop inflated and unrealistic expectations about winning literary prizes. Why worry? My rule of thumb is: Can I earn enough money selling this story to write the next one?

Newspaper reporting taught me that today's story is tomorrow's garbage. It also taught me to define a story quickly, get to the nub of it in as few words as possible, and to find a story in unpromising circumstances. I once despaired at being assigned to cover a convention of librarians, but as the day wore on, I detected a whiff of controversy. I rounded up four or five librarians and fired questions at them. They were articulate and opinionated, and my story made the front page.

At the *Tribune* I also got a crack at local television and drama criticism. I was blunt, and my whack 'em in the head style provoked cries of outrage. Older writers cautioned me to learn to write with a stiletto, not a blunderbuss. I looked around, and I saw a lot of people writing with stilettos. Nobody paid much attention to them. I was the only kid out there with a blunderbuss, and boy, people paid attention to me! I stuck to my guns.

Trust your instincts. If you feel the criticism you receive is stupid or destructive, ignore it. When I began to research *Reservations Are for Indians* in 1966, I approached a prominent Canadian publisher. He listened to my story about poverty on Indian reserves and discontent among native leaders, then shook his head. "Boring," he said. "Nobody wants to read about Indians." When the book was published by Lorimer in 1970, it sold 20,000 copies in six weeks. It is still in print, and public interest in aboriginal issues is still growing.

Writing is manual labour. I compare it to breaking rock in a granite quarry. Whether you use a computer or pen and paper, writing is a struggle. It requires stamina, self-discipline, and, preferably, solitude, although when I was a summer student at the *Winnipeg Free Press* in 1963, I learned I could write in a crowded room amid a din of typewriters, telephones, and editors bellowing "Copy! Copy!" Later, when my son was born and I worked at home, I wrote during odd hours arranged around babysitters and nap times. I have always had a home office, usually a spare bedroom, but you can write anywhere, on a plane or train, in a café, in the basement or in bed, wherever you feel comfortable.

Writing is a discipline. Try to begin at a particular time every day, or to write for a certain number of hours, or stick at it until you have achieved a designated number of pages. You don't have to be in the mood. I have often done my best work when I started out feeling tired and uninspired. Be prepared to stare at the blank page for a long time. I try not to make phone calls while I'm writing, but I love it when the phone rings. Since I work at home, I do my shopping and other chores on weekends or in the afternoons after I've quit. If I am really flying, or working against deadline, those chores don't get done at all. I become so preoccupied that I walk past friends on the street without seeing them. So much for my social life.

Writing should be enjoyable, if only in a monastic or masochistic way. You should find satisfaction in watching your sentences build into paragraphs and pages, feel delight at finding an apt phrase or image, be astonished at words and insights that seem to appear on the page spontaneously. Your research should be so much fun you don't want to stop (see Chapter 2).

Samuel Johnson once observed: "I wonder that so many people have written who might have let it alone." Ask yourself: Is print the best medium for me? My father, Harry, tried to keep journals at several points in his life. He'd buy a scribbler and dutifully fill ten pages or so before giving up. Writing takes a tremendous amount of time, and he lived too intensely in the present to care much for reflection. However, he enjoyed taking photographs of family, friends, and places that were important to him. He invested in a good camera, a tripod, and a timer that allowed him to get into the picture himself, and he left a unique, creative record of his life.

You may prefer to correspond via e-mail, make a video or a quilt, write a song, paint a picture, or record stories on tape. There is nothing magical or mysterious about writing true stories. You don't have to pierce your body, join a cult, smoke dope, or find "the writer within." Trust your judgement.

A writer with common sense will use plain speech and avoid jargon, unless jargon is part of your story or spoken by someone you quote. You can, however, invent your own jargon. You can invent anything: a diet, a philosophy, a religion, a scheme to make money, a formula for suicide. Your story can change a civilization, or vanish without a trace (although I understand discarded books have a long life in landfills).

Be honest. Use the words you think, speak, or hear. This is harder than it sounds (see Chapter 4). If you use "gender" when you mean "sex," you will sound like a government pamphlet. A generation of feminist writers has been wiped out by the gender virus, business writers by corpspeak and bizbabble. We all labour under censorship and self-censorship. The oldest, most ubiquitous, protean, and expressive word in English today is fuck, but it rarely gets a peep in publication.

Have confidence in your voice. Canadian English, with its regional inflections, idioms, and multiple linguistic origins, offers wonderful opportunities for telling stories, yet, at the same time, words cannot always be written the way they sound unless they degenerate into gibberish.

The stories you write will be determined by the stories you read, or the stories you used to read as a child. What do you read? Newspapers? Magazines? True crime? Travel? Biography? I grew up on a diet of *Treasure Island*, my father's stories of prairie history, my mother's Scots and Saskatchewan family lore, W. O. Mitchell's CBC Radio series, "Jake and the Kid," the "Maggie Muggins" stories told on the CBC by Just Mary, and later, the novels of Margaret Laurence. When I reread my own stories, I hear echoes of all these voices.

If you don't read, don't write. Reading will have taught you most of what you need to know. A computer can check your spelling if necessary, and a thesaurus will enlarge your vocabulary (this may not be a good thing). If you feel nervous about grammar, or insecure in English, a style guide will help, but don't rely on a writing course, or a guidebook, even this one, to teach you how to write.

There is a prevalent prejudice that true stories are easier to write, and less creative, than short stories, or fiction. Ignore this. There are two kinds of stories, good and bad. The conventions and disciplines of writing narrative and fiction are equal, but different. In her introduction to her *Selected Stories*, Mavis Gallant calls it "the difference between without and within." She says: "Journalism recounts as exactly and economically as possible the weather in the street; fiction takes no notice of that particular weather but brings to life a distillation of all weathers, a climate of the mind."

There is more boring, badly written fiction published than good fiction; the same is true of non-fiction. I try to avoid the term "non-fiction." It's a negative, meaningless word that fails to acknowledge the variety of narrative forms, and it implies that fiction, a recent populist innovation in the history of literature, sets the standard. Phooey. Tacking "creative" on to "non-fiction" doesn't help.

To write true stories, you need curiosity, an excellent memory, keen eyesight, and a sensitive ear for the rhythms and nuances of conversation. It also helps to have a *nose* for a story, that little twitch, the scent of blood, that says: "Gotcha!" Shy people make good reporters because they are good listeners. Where you live doesn't matter: Paul Theroux took a train to Patagonia, E. B. White contemplated his pig.

If you didn't announce to your parents at the age of six, "I'm going to be a writer!" don't worry. Not many kids do. Writers work at other things, and all kinds of people write. Lawyers write. Mathematicians, physicists, and philosophers write. Cancer patients keep journals, Holocaust survivors publish memoirs, auto workers become experts on family history. Many people don't begin to write until they retire.

I started writing professionally, if you call it that, for the student newspaper at the University of Manitoba. In my innocence, I discovered that *anyone* could write for *The Manitoban*, even me, as long as I turned up once or twice a week for the press nights, and since there were always desperate last-minute holes to fill, I could write anything I wanted. The university had no journalism school, so the paper was run by a mix of political wannabes, beatniks, English majors, Rhodes scholars, medical students, architect/cartoonists, Hungarian refugees, and comedians from the law school. We taught ourselves to type.

The Manitoban was *the* place to hang out, and since my parents thought I was doing something literary, on press nights they allowed me to stay out until dawn. They thought I was studying English literature to become a professor. So did I, until I became editor of *The Manitoban* and discovered the power of the written word.

My first issues came out in the autumn of 1961. I had no expectation of notoriety. The campus was small, about three thousand students. Most of them were young men in science, engineering, and agriculture, and if they picked up the paper at all, they used it to mop up their spilled coffee in the student cafeteria. I knew, because we all had to walk through the crap in the caf to reach *The Manitoban* offices on the second floor. The rest of the students' union building, a decrepit airplane hangar left over from the war, housed the council and committee offices, a gymnasium, and the athletic department.

It was a firetrap, a hard place to work, or work out, a squalid monument to the university's high-minded indifference to extracurricular activities. Or so we thought, until the university decided to fund an intercollegiate football team. In an editorial, I denounced the team as an irresponsible waste of money. I considered my views reasonable, and so did the athletic director, until I was summoned to a meeting of the student council to explain why I shouldn't be fired.

As I sat in the council chamber in the airplane hangar, next to the deserted cafeteria, waiting to defend myself, I became aware of a low, murmuring roar outside. I looked out the window. A mob of guys in athletic jackets was milling around the quadrangle. There was a platform, and someone was shouting into a microphone. The roar, punctuated by screams and bellows, rose and fell as he spoke, and as it reached a crescendo, I saw a lifesize, straw-stuffed scarecrow being hoisted up a pole. It may have had hair, or a skirt, but as I watched it swinging from a rope, I thought: "Hey, that's me."

I kept my job – the student politicians were horrified by the uproar outside – and by the time I left the building only a few guys were still hanging around. I walked past them towards the parking lot, nervous, but too angry to be afraid. A few faces turned towards me, their expressions opaque, indifferent, then turned away again.

The calm was disconcerting. Had I imagined the whole scene? Then it hit me: "They don't recognize me! They've hanged me, and they don't even know who I am!" I laughed all the way home. I knew then that nothing else I could do with my life would ever be this exciting.

FURTHER READING

Pierre Berton, *The National Dream* (1970) and *The Last Spike* (1971), McClelland & Stewart. Berton's strength is his ability to develop his characters and put them in motion. He writes about the rich and powerful without being obsequious.

Norman Mailer, *Pieces and Pontifications*, Little, Brown. Thirty years ago, I read almost everything Mailer wrote. Now I wonder why.

Andrew Morton, *Diana: Her True Story*, Simon & Schuster. Morton scored the astonishing coup of publishing Diana's debunking story about the royals in 1992, then cashing in on her myth with an updated postmortem version in 1997. Morton's primary source was Diana herself. Fleet Street at its best.

Paul Theroux, *The Old Patagonian Express*, Pocket Books, 1979. Theroux has also written an earlier book about travelling on the Trans-Siberian railroad, and many subsequent travel stories. He has his fans, but I find his manner pompous, his attitudes snobbish and sexist. Not a guy I want to share a seat with.

CHAPTER 2

Digging and Talking

Teachers often tell beginning writers, "Write what you know." This is useless advice, since it is by writing that we discover what we know. Writing is as much a learning experience for me as for my readers. I almost always end a book or a magazine story in a place I never expected to be when I began, and I am constantly surprised by the phrases and images that appear on my screen as I type. Where did that idea come from? Do I *really* think that?

Taken too literally, what we "know" is the daily routine of our lives, our relationships with family and friends, our jobs, joys, and disappointments. Unless there is something exceptional or dramatic about these circumstances, or you have the talent of an E. B. White or Erma Bombeck, they are unpromising material for true stories. Remember that boring, predictable school essay: "What I Did on My Summer Holidays"?

There is no rule that says you have to confine your interests to yourself, or to your own race, culture, or community. Many writers, including me, choose offbeat, unfamiliar topics. Write *what you want to know.*

Story ideas are all around us, and fresh ones present themselves every day. Writers and editors scour newspapers and magazines and haunt the television news, looking for an event or an image that triggers that little *ping* of curiosity. A story can come from anywhere: chance conversations, memories, a personal interest or emotional reaction, a theory. Your story may be right in front of your face. Psychologist Betty Friedan, stuck at home with three kids, began interviewing other disgruntled housewives, and her research led to *The Feminine Mystique*. Another tactic is to take a conventional story and turn it on its head. For instance, if you're tired of reading about battered wives, write a story about women who beat up their husbands. Your story doesn't have to be news; many conventional stories succeed because they are well-written.

If you feel you have a good idea, scrutinize it. How long should this story be? Who will publish it? Read it? Can I afford the time and the expense of doing it? Analyze the ingredients. What is *new* about this person or event? Is there drama? Confrontation? A hint of mystery or immorality? Why do I like this idea? Will I like it six weeks from now? Discuss your idea with trusted friends or family members. If their eyes glaze over, take the hint. On the other hand, if their eyes pop out and they squawk, "Are you nuts?" feel encouraged. Do some preliminary research. Will the sources you need be accessible? Many good ideas founder because documents have been destroyed or locked up, relatives are hostile, or the key players won't talk. You may find that one or two other writers have already staked out the ground. Can you compete with the paparazzi or pack journalists? Will your story be old hat before it's written?

Before you begin your research, think about what form your story will take. Will it be biography, social history, true crime, documentary? The shape may change, depending on what you discover. One story I thought was a magazine feature grew into a book – the feature never did get written – and more than one feature idea has ended up as a column. Having a framework, however, will help you direct your search and shape the raw material for your story as you assemble it.

Cast your net wide. Although your story may be short, your research must be comprehensive. The one contact you ignore, the one phone call you neglect, may be the most important. If you are writing a memoir or autobiography, for instance, look beyond your own collection of scrapbooks, letters, and photographs. Friends, colleagues, and family members may have memorabilia to contribute, as well as their own points of view, and referring to public sources such as contemporary magazines and newspapers will put your story in context and refresh your memory.

Never take anything for granted. Assuming that we know something to be true is the most common mistake journalists make. Check it out. Look it up. *Ask.* You'll be appalled how often you're wrong.

Accept nothing at face value. Corroborate your information from several sources. Interviews are generally regarded as less factually reliable than print, and various witnesses to events will have different versions. If, for instance, you are writing a profile of someone in the news, don't limit your research to this person's cronies. Find some critics. Journalists are often manipulated into writing phoney stories because they print all the crud they're fed.

Don't allow yourself to be used by someone with a personal grievance or malicious motives. If, for instance, Joe Smith says very critical things about John Brown, don't print his comments before confirming them with Brown. You don't have to tell Brown your source, simply give him a chance to respond to the criticism. Don't believe Brown either – find letters, contracts, or testimony that will prove the allegations.

Resist the urge to guess, invent, or censor your information. The temptation to manipulate a story to fit the way we *want* it to turn out, or the way an editor wants it to turn out, can be overwhelming, and don't allow the people in your story to bully you into writing it *their* way. Don't suck. Keep an open mind. Follow where your research leads. Write the story the way it *is*. It's tough, but you'll end up with a better story.

Don't worry about being objective. Stories are as often badly distorted in the name of "fairness" and "balance" (i.e., what the publisher thinks) as they are for political or personal reasons. It's a smart idea to present all sides of an issue to heighten drama and conflict, but a writer has no obligation to include dull or irrelevant material. Let the facts, and the people, speak for themselves.

"Research" has a bad reputation it doesn't deserve. It tends to be associated with "scholarly," and conjures up images of pale, frowzy people hunched over piles of mouldy papers. This is true, but only partly, and a scholarly book doesn't have to be boring or badly written – think of Simone de Beauvoir, Germaine Greer, John Kenneth Galbraith, and Stephen Hawking. Journalists research, at least the good ones do, and in most archives family historians outnumber the professional scholars.

Research is a good excuse to travel and talk to interesting people you would otherwise never meet. It can involve investigating old buildings, examining paintings or photographs, reading diaries and personal letters, or surfing the Internet. Research takes time and perseverance. It can be frustrating, infuriating, exhilarating. I enjoy research as much as writing, for different reasons, and some people become so addicted they never stop to write their story.

Skimpy, sloppy research shows. Your story will be superficial, full of omissions and riddled with errors. You will likely miss the point. You will repeat a lot of misinformation you have picked up from other lazy writers, and they will recycle all your mistakes because they can't be bothered to check. Readers will swallow all this bumf – it's a true story, isn't it? – and develop false opinions and skewed ideas. Much of what passes for history and biography is slop. It drives me crazy. Research is essential. Do it.

How? And where to begin? Imagine yourself as Sherlock Holmes, or a prospector panning for gold. Sift a river of gravel to find the nuggets, watch for the clue that will solve your puzzle. I tend to work on the vacuum cleaner principle – suck up everything, read it, sort it, and wait to see what sticks in my mind. I often find that images and bits of information I at first dismiss as inconsequential become the focus of my story. This is scary. What if I hadn't taken notes, or saved those stray scraps of paper? Don't expect to find your story sitting in the middle of the road. Look for it hiding in the ditch, crouching under a culvert, or hanging from an overhead wire.

Be methodical. Don't rush off in a frenzy of enthusiasm and do everything backwards. A good story is organic. It takes time to germinate, and demands careful cultivation to grow to maturity. A blunder at the beginning can blight your whole project, or kill it entirely.

Sources are usually divided into "primary" and "secondary." A signed letter is considered a primary source; a magazine story is secondary. The difference is one of weight and credibility. Sworn testimony or a legal document such as a will has greater authority than information that has been processed by an intermediary, an obituary for instance. The line can be blurry. Early census returns, for example, are treated as primary sources, but the census taker was a writer capable of misspelling names and mistaking boys for girls. Is a gravestone a primary or secondary source? The inscription wasn't carved by the deceased, and the stone may have been moved from its original location.

Be suspicious. People lie, and perjure themselves on the witness stand. Simply because your grandmother told you, or you read it in the *New York Times*, doesn't mean it's necessarily true. Even letters can be suspect. In 1964, historian Marc La Terreur donated to the

National Archives of Canada a package of fragmentary letters purportedly written by Sir Wilfrid Laurier, prime minister of Canada from 1896 to 1911, to his mistress, Émilie Lavergne. The letters were incomplete. They had no dates or salutations and Émilie is never mentioned by name. They were unsigned, or signed only "W. L." La Terreur had received the letters from Émilie's nephew, Renaud. The Archives photocopied them, and accepted La Terreur's word that they were authentic.

In 1967, La Terreur abruptly reclaimed the letters, allowing the Archives to keep the copies. In 1971, shortly after La Terreur was killed in an accident, the letters were offered for sale by a Montreal antique dealer who advertised them as "among the most beautiful love letters I have ever read." Charles Fisher, a rare book collector, bought them and published them in 1989 as *Dearest Émilie: The Love Letters of Sir Wilfrid Laurier to Madame Émilie Lavergne*. Fisher locked the originals in his vault.

The photocopies I read suggest that the letters were written by Laurier, but not all of them necessarily to Émilie, and someone other than Laurier appears to have pencilled in dates and Laurier's initials. For love letters, they are remarkably dispassionate. Laurier never calls Émilie anything more intimate than "dearest friend." She *was* a dear friend. A lover? I doubt it. The tone of the letters struck me as false, and their strange history bothered me. What had happened to the rest of this correspondence? Why had Émilie not sold these letters herself, or given them to the Archives? Why had two letters in the sequence turned up in the possession of Laurier's successor as Liberal leader, Mackenzie King? Had Émilie tried blackmail?

It is common for heirs and executors to destroy, annotate, and edit the private papers entrusted to their care. Information is not true simply because it is in print. Government documents show bias; the minutes of a meeting may omit most of what was said.

Archives, of course, are only one of innumerable sources, and sources inevitably lead to others you may never have heard about. Experienced researchers learn how to go quickly to the most important primary information, the horse's mouth so to speak, but if you feel intimidated, or fearful of being lost in the swamp, start slowly.

Circle in on your story. Begin with the most obvious secondary sources: books, periodicals, and newspapers. Check the catalogue at your local library to see what it has in your subject area. (If you are unsure how to use the video terminal, ask for help – libraries have different computer systems.) Discuss your interest with a librarian. The library may have clipping files, photographs, or a special collection that is not on display, and a good librarian will suggest other sources.

The most important parts of any book or article you read are the notes and bibliography. Here you will find the sources this writer has used, and you can follow up those you find interesting. They will, in turn, lead to more sources, and your paper chase is underway.

Cruise the shelves of the biggest urban bookstore you can find. You may discover that someone else has just published the book you are planning to write, or that there are five new books on the same topic. Don't despair. There always seems to be room for another book about how to get rich quick, survive illness, or find happiness. Books by, and about, women have had a good run for more than thirty years. Booksellers like titles they can group together under signs like "Holistic" or "Business." They hate orphan books on unfamiliar topics, although these may be the most original. If you feel your story has been done, can you give your idea a fresh slant? Change history to biography? Don't worry about competition: books on similar topics sell each other. At worst, you've saved yourself a lot of wasted effort.

If you find that almost nothing significant has been published, you're either ahead of the pack or you've run into a wall. Literature has fashions, and publishing is rife with prejudice. You won't see a bookstore shelf labelled "Poverty" because poor people don't write or buy books, and anything that looks too "ethnic" is shunned because the target market is small. Writing and reading is a middle-class pursuit, and only a fragment of our experience is reflected in our literature. Fashions change, however. Old age, once a big topic with the Greeks, is coming back: the middle class is aging, and the aging have more money than the young.

If you encounter a *tabula rasa*, look at your project with a cold, critical eye. Can you commit time and effort to something which may never be published? Will you find enough source material for your research? How confident are you in the strength of your story? I've jumped off this cliff a few times and survived. Trust your gut instinct. If *you* find your idea exciting, other people may too, and you will have the fun of digging in unexplored territory. It is, however, a hard slog through the unmapped boulders and muskeg of primary sources.

Slogging can be literally true, especially if you are writing a travel book. The most primary source is the place, person, or object you are writing about. Let's say you intend to write an illustrated history of sailing ships on the Great Lakes. Initial reading should give you an idea of the towns where these ships were built, or a shipyard or museum where you might still find one. (A few wrecks are accessible to scuba divers at the bottom of the lakes.)

Go there. You may find an enterprise still going strong, manufacturing something completely different, or descendants of the original builders who live in town. Look around at the waterfront. Does it reflect its history, or has it been built up with casinos and condos? Can you describe this place in an interesting way? Check in at the local library and museum. They will likely have company records, local histories, self-published memoirs, photographs, memorabilia, and artefacts.

Every community has a local history society and an amateur historian. Their strength tends to be oral history, or gossip. They can be very helpful. For instance, you might learn that the town was a smugglers' haven during the nineteenth century, and the great-granddaughter of the most successful smuggler is the president of the society. They will also have stories about storms, shipwrecks, drownings and other disasters, as well as everything you need to know about family feuds and the private lives of all the important people in town.

Explain clearly to the people you meet who you are and the information you are looking for. They will suggest new leads. Note them, with the names of key contact people, addresses, phone and fax numbers. Leave a business card, or write down your own name and number, and move on. Don't dig a deep hole in one corner of the field until you have scouted the lay of the land.

As you follow your leads to new sources, assess their scope and quality. Are files neatly organized, or will you have to paw through cardboard boxes full of unsorted papers? Are the contact people knowledgeable and cooperative? Is history fresh in people's minds? Will key people be willing to talk to you?

Keep in mind that you are looking for an object: a ship. You can't write about all the ships that have sailed the Great Lakes; you have to choose particular ships. Your ship may turn out to be famous or obscure, a ship that brought United Empire Loyalists from New York State to Canada, or took Irish immigrants along the shore of Lake Ontario to York. It may have fought in the War of 1812, or been part of a fleet that carried wheat from Canada to the United States. It may be a racing yacht, a rowboat, or a three-masted schooner. It is a ship with a story.

Your search will take you to the Archives of Ontario, the

National Archives of Canada, the Toronto Marine Museum and City of Toronto Archives, the Royal Canadian Yacht Club, several Great Lakes ports in Canada and the United States, and possibly to New York City, Washington, D.C., and Great Britain. You will find the threads of your inquiry leading into the lumber industry, trade and commerce, war, rebellion, international affairs, customs and tariffs, food, furniture, weather, and aboriginal culture (sails replaced hides and bark in the making of tents).

Use the ship to tell your story. You may get no closer than a painting or a photograph, but with diligence you should be able to find representative ships rich with association and anecdote, and a wealth of drawings, etchings, sketches, and other illustrations. Set yourself a deadline to complete your research, even if you have to break it, and try to set aside chunks of research time to avoid losing concentration. Don't forget the people who sailed on your ship: the captain and crew, cabin and steerage passengers, soldiers, oarsmen, and stowaways. You may be keen on construction and design; your book's appeal to most readers will be the stories it tells about people.

Research demands courage and diplomacy. You have to approach all kinds of strangers, introduce yourself and ask for their cooperation. You will encounter the occasional rebuff – a snotty curator, a rude relative – but your main problem will be indifference. Who are you, and why do you want to know all this stuff? Be polite, but tenacious. Give people plenty of time to produce the information you want. Establish trust. Be prepared to return to a source many times. Remember, this is a safe you have to crack, and they have the code.

Don't try to get blood from a stone. But if a good source dries up, or a contact is obstructionist, ask yourself: "Are these people withholding information? Why? Do they have something to hide?" Look for gaps in the records. What's missing? Why? These questions may set you on a new path that leads to the heart of your story. Silence is information in itself.

It's unfortunate that our collective memory tends to be stored in former jails, or buildings that look like jails, churches, or hospitals. These are archives, and yes, archives *are* open to the public, usually for free. Major archives remain open in the evenings and on weekends for greater accessibility. Once you pull open the heavy door, and check in with the security guard, you will likely find yourself in a busy, stimulating environment surrounded by qualified experts who are glad you are there.

Ask for help. Indexes and finding aids can be intimidating, and I have often found that a ten-minute chat with an archivist has saved me hours of rooting in the wrong places. You may want to phone ahead, establish contact with an expert in your field and arrange a time to visit. An archivist can point you in the direction you want to go, save you weeks of research time, and provide you with material you otherwise might never discover.

Plan to spend time searching the archive's collection, and in large archives, expect delays while books and documents are retrieved from storage. If you have to travel a long way, do as much preliminary research as possible by phone, fax, e-mail, and the Internet. Most major libraries and archives have Web sites, and if you don't have the computer technology at home, many community centres and copy shops will provide access to this service for a fee. You may be able to do most of your research electronically, although, for me, nothing beats getting my hands on *the real thing*. Even if you are not a university graduate, university libraries, archives, and rare book collections are also accessible to the public. I pay one hundred dollars a year for full library privileges at the University of Toronto. It's one of the best investments I've ever made.

If your story is contemporary, or set in the recent past, you have the opportunity to interview people who are, or have been, part of the action. Interviews tend to fall into two categories. The first is "just the facts, ma'am," a short conversation seeking information or confirmation. The second is the personality interview, an encounter with a person who is crucial to your story. This interview may take hours. The facts are secondary. You want to capture this person's character and history, memories, anecdotes, observations, opinions and points of view.

Getting inside another person's head requires self-effacement, empathy, and acute attention to nuances and clues. Prepare. Research everything you can find by or about this person. Don't flaunt your expertise – if you know more than they do, you shouldn't be there – but people feel reassured when you have done your homework.

Never be afraid to ask a dumb question. The simple, honest question is the most effective, and encourages people to speak in ordinary language. So what if you look stupid? Your sole purpose is to get this person to *spill the beans*. Good interviewers radiate innocence, sympathy, and understanding even when they're thinking, "Wow, is this guy a jerk!"

Interviews lead to new sources and help confirm facts, but their greatest value is anecdotal. Quotations take the place of dialogue in fiction. They add fresh perspectives and a variety of voices to your narrative. Natural storytellers with colloquial and imaginative ways of speaking are uncommon, but most interviews will yield at least one good quote.

The hardest part of an interview is making the call. What if your quarry says no, and slams down the phone? This rarely happens. Most people are flattered to be interviewed and happy to share their knowledge. Don't bother writing a formal letter of request. No one feels obliged to respond to a letter from a stranger. A phone call establishes immediate rapport and gives you both a chance to discuss your project. If you feel your quarry is likely to be reluctant, go through an intermediary who can vouch for your trustworthiness. If it is necessary to write a letter, close by saying that you will follow up with a phone call.

If your quarry is evasive, take your time. Don't pester, but don't give up right away. You may think of a way of approaching them that will pique their interest. Never misrepresent yourself or your project, and give the same explanation to everyone you meet. They will compare notes. If you give one person the impression that you are a student writing a thesis, and the next person thinks you're a journalist, everyone will become suspicious and clam up.

They will clam up if they think you're an idiot. Never do an interview until you know who this person is, and have at least a basic grasp of your subject. Ask yourself: "Why do I want to talk to *this* person? What are they likely to tell me? How will it contribute to my story?" List a few essential questions. Don't waste everybody's time on a fishing expedition.

You can do a good interview on the phone, often on your first call. The phone encourages confidences, and if your quarry is in a hurry, they might blurt out things they would not say to your face. However, if you would like to build this person into a character in your story, make an appointment to see them in person. Encourage them to set the time, and to invite you into their home or office. People feel more comfortable on their own turf, and you have the opportunity to describe their appearance and surroundings. A famous hostess may have ashtrays full of cigarette butts; a Wall Street stockbroker may work out of an office done up like Dracula's castle. Avoid restaurants: they are cramped and noisy and it's hard to eat and talk at the same time.

If possible, interview each person alone. In a group, everyone tends to talk at once, and shy people may not say a word. In private,

people will often tell you secrets they won't reveal in the presence
of others. Don't pretend that an interview is a casual chat. It's a
solemn contract. You are asking this person for a gift, and you
intend to make this gift public. You expect them to tell the truth,
and they expect you to reproduce it accurately.

How people convey information is as important as the information itself. Keep an eye peeled for details you can use to bring
this person to life in print – an unusual voice, striking gestures or
mannerisms, idiosyncrasies of appearance – as long as these relate
to your theme. Body language offers many clues to personality.
Don't forget your own body language. A jumpy or abrasive manner
will create tension. Sit quietly, make eye contact, and *smile*.

An interview requires etiquette. Do not offer money or bring a
gift – most people would be insulted. If your quarry demands
payment, you have to assess the value of the transaction. If this is a
hot story for the popular press, your editor or publisher may think
a large fee is worth it. It's unlikely that $50 or $500 will buy anything worth printing. Don't blithely promise people a share of your
fee or royalties unless you sign a written agreement approved
by your lawyer and publisher. Payment inflates the value of what
might turn out to be a worthless or marginal contribution, and
many people have exaggerated ideas of the amount of money to be
made by writing. I don't pay.

What if someone insists on talking "off the record"? Try to talk
them out of it. It may be false modesty, or that their fears are exaggerated. Anonymous sources weaken your story. On the other
hand, their revelations may be sensational. If you feel it's worth the
trouble, go ahead. You can include this information indirectly, or
use it to persuade someone else to talk on the record. Off-the-
record sources are most annoying when you badly need to quote
them. Readers distrust phrases like "a senior executive" or "a
former prostitute." In these cases, I use a pseudonym. Make sure

you tell the reader that it *is* a pseudonym. If you do promise anonymity, *keep that promise.* Reveal this person's identity to no one, including the police or a court of law, even if you go to jail.

Now that you have your foot in the door, don't spook your host. A writer I know turned up for a 9:00 a.m. interview reeking of whisky. He was thrown out. However, if your host suggests a drink, oblige (it doesn't have to be whisky). It may be the start of a wonderful conversation. Don't worry if you are young and inexperienced. Being patronized can be hard to swallow, but when people don't take you seriously, their guard will be down. Who wants to be interviewed by Mike Wallace?

Be on time. This interview is important to both of you. Wear your everyday clothes – writers are expected to look like writers – but dress in a way appropriate to your host's expectations. Remove your muddy shoes and pat the dog. Don't expect to be fed, and if your host smokes, put up with it. Remember that you are a stranger, and your host may be more nervous than you are.

Ask people where they like to sit. It's usually easy to spot a favourite chair, but many people prefer the kitchen table. Carry your weapon – your notebook or tape recorder – in full view, or produce it as soon as you sit down. I use a tape recorder only if people speak very quickly, or in idiosyncratic language. Scribbling their answers to my questions gives me time to think of the next question, and silence encourages people to keep talking.

What if they don't talk? It's your fault. Never ask a question that can be answered "yes" or "no." Don't ask: "Did you go to bible college in California?" Ask: "Where did you go to bible college?" Don't ask a question that answers itself: "Gee, it must have felt great to score that winning goal?" Ask: "Hey, how did you deke that guy out of the net?" Never assume that you know what someone is thinking, as in: "I'm sure your thoughts are with your husband on this space mission." Oh yeah? She may be glad he's out of the way.

Don't turn a statement of opinion into a question: "Isn't this harassment of the president's wife a disgrace?"

Suppress your own opinions. You don't want to start an argument and antagonize your source. If people think you have an agenda, they will play to your prejudices and tell you what they think you want to know. It may be helpful, however, to express encouragement: "Isn't that interesting!" Do not encourage them to give their opinions unless that is the purpose of your interview; people have all kinds of hobby horses and once they ride off it can be impossible to get them back.

Arrive prepared with three or four questions you hope will lead in revealing directions. *Listen.* If an answer veers off in a completely unexpected direction, go with the flow. A phrase or an image will provide a follow-up question. Ask for clarification. Try to figure out where this stream of memory is taking you – your questions may be answered long before you get a chance to ask them. If you find yourself in a backwater, or the answers are going in circles, tactfully interrupt with a question that leads in a fresh direction.

Remember your Sherlock Holmes hat. These people are witnesses. Ask them questions about *their own experience*, what *they* saw, heard, and did. Avoid hearsay. If you say something like: "The Simpsons, who lived down the street, weren't they a little strange?" you might get: "Simpsons? Didn't know them very well. Hair was a little unusual. Had a couple of kids. Moved away, years ago, heard one of the kids was killed, don't know when. Fred next door might know, why don't you talk to Fred?" Interviews that drift wreck on the shoals of irrelevance.

Let's say you are writing a story about an eccentric millionaire, Gertrude Beeblefetz, and you've tracked down Mimi, a cook who worked for Beeblefetz for thirty years. If you ask: "You must have known Ms. Beeblefetz well, what was she like?" Mimi will probably reply: "Oh, a little eccentric." But if you ask: "What did you cook for Ms. Beeblefetz? What food did she enjoy?" Mimi may reply: "Well, Trudy always had liver for lunch. She enjoyed that, fresh liver, calves' liver, rare. Healthy, she said. She was concerned about her heart. No onions. Her dog didn't like onions. She always fed the scraps to the dog. Under the table, the dog was. A large dog, one of those kind that kill people. Rip your throat right out. Never bothered me, but mind you I didn't wait on table. Have you spoken to Geoffrey, the butler? I think I have his number . . ." Now you have an anecdote, a dozen more questions, and a new source directly connected to your topic.

Listen to the voice as well as to the words. Pick up on emotion. Ask about feelings: "How did you feel when you lost your job?" Releasing suppressed emotions can unleash a torrent of startling anecdotes. You may have heard, or assumed from photographs, that a famous woman grew up in a happy, close-knit family. If you say: "Tell me about your wonderful family," she will respond with banalities. If you ask: "What did your family think of your decision to study medicine?" you may discover that she'd had a bitter fight with her father.

Listen for what is unsaid. Let silence speak. Resist the urge to babble. Wait. Note the blanks and try to fill them in later. Why is this person reluctant to discuss this issue? Raise the question with other sources: "I noticed your sister seemed a little reluctant to talk about her years in Africa." You might uncover an unhappy love affair, illness, or professional failure. On the other hand, she may have nothing to say about Africa.

People often talk obliquely, or in parables. If someone keeps coming back to a topic that appears irrelevant, there may be a reason. I once interviewed a woman who kept retelling the story of her mother's death. I could see no connection to my questions, but as she added more detail, I came to understand, although she never spoke the word, that her mother had died of tuberculosis. Tuberculosis *was* a theme in my story. Her obliqueness told me that TB had been taboo, and the memory of her mother's death, decades earlier, remained almost unspeakably painful.

Screw up your courage to ask the really difficult questions. You may anticipate hostility, but people who have been victimized, or involved in controversy, may be happy to set the record straight. When I was researching a book on the Canadian prime ministers' wives, I arranged, through a mutual friend, to interview Maureen McTeer. Her husband, Joe Clark, had been prime minister from 1979 to 1980, and McTeer, a young woman with a sharp tongue and strong opinions, had been given a rough ride by the media. I was media. I was apprehensive, and a week or so before the interview, I had been told on good authority that McTeer and Clark were getting divorced. How was I going to handle this?

McTeer didn't cancel, and when I turned up at their house, everything looked relaxed and domestic. What was going on? I steered the conversation towards the homey decor, and McTeer began to explain why she and Joe, who was still a cabinet minister, kept their private lives separate from their public roles.

"Those who dislike us are still using things against me in an attempt to bring Joe down," she said. "It's *painfully* obvious, it's very stressful, and it's very distressing to our family. I am always getting divorced. For the past seventeen years, every year I have been getting a divorce. Society is so conditioned politically now to judge people exclusively by their personal life. They don't deal with issues any more, just gossip, that is the way we bring people down. My own gardener said, 'Oh, I'm so sorry, Ms. McTeer.' 'What?' 'I was just told you were getting divorced.' I said, 'I don't know, am I?' This is crazy, the gardener is telling *me* I'm getting divorced!"

I had to resist the urge to hug her. McTeer had saved me the embarrassment of having to ask *the* question, scotched a rumour, told a lively anecdote, revealed a good deal about her personality, and shared an intimate insight into her life. And she had earned my respect.

People will tell you exactly what they want to tell you, nothing more. We have a finite number of stories we are prepared to share with others. Our story sack may be small and homespun, or large and embroidered, but once it's empty, that's it. People tell the same stories over and over, and no amount of badgering or cajoling will make any difference. The best you can do is empty the sack.

A good interview demands energy, concentration, memory, and the ability to think about many things at once. I often feel I am *willing* people to tell me what I need to know. I ask a question, listen attentively to the answer while recording it, plan the next question, assess all the information I have been told, keep an ear cocked for nuance, and worry about what I've forgotten to ask while giving this person my undivided attention. Add anxiety and an adrenalin rush, and I end a good interview exhausted.

What if the person starts spilling the beans after you've put your notebook away? This often happens. I take my notebook out again, or if that's inconvenient I memorize as much as I can and write the sentences out in the car, or repeat key words and phrases until I can record what I remember when I get home. What if they say, "Oh, don't print *this*!"? To hell with them. Interviews don't have to be done with notes or tapes, but be careful not to make factual mistakes, or present your unrecorded material in a way that will provoke a law suit. In an interview setting, everything the subject says or does is fair game.

Unless you're hired to ghost an autobiography, never agree to show your subjects your notes or draft manuscript. It's your story, not theirs. Few people ask, but if they do, I assure them that I, or an independent checker, will confirm their facts and quotes by fax or phone. Once the interview is in the bag, there's not much they can do about it.

Close your interviews by thanking people. Ask if they have anything more they'd like to say, or if they know of other resources. Your Ali Baba may have been guarding his cave for fifty years, waiting for you to say the magic words. Always ask for more names. This person will now have some idea of what you're after, and if you've hit it off, may help pave your way. Respect the grapevine. If you are credible and trusted, your most important sources may come to you.

CHAPTER 3

The Story: What Happened?
Who Cares?

I begin to write when I am bored asking questions. Puzzles are solved, I get the same information from different sources, and my story is taking shape in my mind. Once I start writing, potholes in my narrative will prompt more research, but until then I don't want to waste time digging up a lot of stuff I may never use.

At this point, I acquire a nagging companion who will peer over my shoulder and make rude noises until my manuscript is finished. This is my imaginary reader. Writing is a creative partnership; your story will only have value if someone else reads it. Ask yourself: "Who am I writing for? Who will read this page? Buy this book?" These questions are especially important if you are writing about yourself: Are you really that interesting to anybody else?

I imagine my reader as a bus driver. I have no idea why, and I'm sure I have no great following among bus drivers. A bus driver, however, is a responsible, mass-market, middle-of-the-road image that reminds me I have to step up smartly, pay the exact fare, and share the bus with other riders. My bus driver is the first one to put on the brakes: "Wait a minute! What is all this slush? You fool! We're stuck in the mud! This is a detour – get back in gear!"

The hardest part about writing, as they say, is applying the seat of the pants to the seat of the chair, and, as Truman Capote once said of Jack Kerouac, there is a difference between writing and typing. How do we find it?

Writers work in different ways. Some make detailed outlines, others, like me, jump in. Some forge ahead to complete a rough draft, then edit, revise, and rewrite; I rewrite as I go. I often write in my head. I may be lying in bed or staring out the window, but I'm working hard. The most important part of my work, the sifting, mulling, brooding, imagining, is done when I am not at the computer.

First, place yourself within a literary tradition or genre. Is this a memoir? History? A travel story? Polemic? It may be a combination of several, but emphasize one. The genre you choose will provide an architect's model, a prefab scaffolding you can use to build your house, and a set of appropriate tools. Writing is a craft. Words are bricks, and books are built on other books. A true story is not "real life," it's an imitation, a construct, and we can use all the help we can get.

Is your story a comedy or a tragedy? Romance? Melodrama? Establishing the tone or mood will help bring it into focus. How do you feel? Angry? Nostalgic? Contemplative? How do you want your readers to respond?

Think your story through before you begin to write: What do I want to say? Who are my characters? Where do I begin? What happens? How does it end? A strong ending is as important as a good opening, or "lead" as they say in journalism, and if you're writing a book, every chapter, as well as the book itself, should have a strong beginning, middle, and end.

Shakespeare's plays provide a model that works as well for narrative as it does for drama and screenplays. Think of your story as an arc: exposition, complication, climax, resolution. The ending should flow naturally from events and echo the beginning.

Shakespeare frames the tragedy of King Lear between two scenes involving the earls of Kent and Gloucester and Gloucester's two sons, Edgar and Edmund. In *Hamlet*, Horatio sees the ghost of Hamlet's father in act I, scene I, and is still on hand to say "Good night, sweet prince," when Hamlet dies at the end of act V.

Shakespeare makes this unity appear effortless. It's not. He uses all kinds of devices – twins, lost children, mistaken identity – and there's nothing like a good murder/suicide for a popular climax. Who knows how many quill pens Will wore out fussing over his structure?

I start thinking about my opening and closing scenes as soon as I commit to the story, and finding them becomes part of my research. In my book about General Motors of Canada, *Driving Force: The McLaughlin Family and the Age of the Car*, I open with a scene in a Buick assembly plant threatened with closure in 1991, and end watching the last van go down the line in a GM plant that shut down in 1993.

Neither choice was accidental. I reconstructed the first scene from interviews, and I twisted a few arms to get into the van plant the day it closed. I had decided on my opening scene early in my research – the impending death of the Canadian-built McLaughlin-Buick car was the inspiration for my book – but the last van was a shot in the dark:

As the van left each section of the plant, the drag chain stopped. The lights were turned off. I walked alone through the plant in the twilight, my footsteps loud on the concrete floor. I could feel the huge skeleton of the beast twitching, warm with grease. Lockers were flung open, tattered Sunshine Girls smirking on their inside doors, and a sign on a supervisor's blackboard read: DEATH TO THE VAN PLANT AND B-SHIFT ASSHOLES!

I came upon blackened pits, the size of communal graves, where welders had worked beneath the vans, their plastic masks glowing in the sparks from their torches. The welders were gone, but they had left behind the homely little chairs they had fashioned out of scrap metal and duct tape. I felt I had stumbled on the tomb of the Industrial Revolution, the bleak world my grandfather had left behind, and as I watched the last, white van bob away in its brilliant bubble of light, I imagined his emigrant ship steaming down the Clyde, the lights of the dying shipyards fading in the mist, and heard in the ripple of the ebbing tide the cadences of Mathew Arnold's great elegy:

> The Sea of Faith
> Was once, too, at the full, and round earth's shore
> Lay like the folds of a bright girdle furl'd.
> But now I only hear,
> Its melancholy, long, withdrawing roar,
> Retreating, to the breath
> Of the night-wind, down the vast edges drear
> And naked shingles of the world.

I didn't finish my book for another two years, but I knew where I was going. I could place myself, the car, and the McLaughlins in the context of the Industrial Revolution and weave these themes and images throughout my story. In my own prose, I occasionally echoed the melancholy oboe notes of Arnold's "Dover Beach."

Find a way to attack your story; don't back into it like a squid in a cloud of ink. Shakespeare gets right down to business. King Lear has barely arrived on stage when he says: "Give me the map there.

Know that we have divided in three our kingdom." Lear then tells his three daughters to speak up, and the play is underway.

A good lead hooks the reader and opens up dramatic opportunities. "He haunts us still" is the memorable first sentence of *Trudeau and Our Times*, by Stephen Clarkson and Christina McCall (McClelland & Stewart), and Isak Dinesen begins *Out of Africa* (Random House, 1937) with this simple, beautiful sentence: "I had a farm in Africa at the foot of the Ngong Hills." If your lead works, the rest of the story will tell itself. Study the opening paragraphs of newspaper and magazine stories. I have chosen two typical examples from the *Globe and Mail*, January 10, 1997.

The first is a front-page story by justice reporter Kirk Makin headlined: "Legal-aid cash squeeze clogs courts." Sounds dull, but Makin's first word, "exasperated," catches my eye. He begins:

> Exasperated after a morning of setting trial dates for an unruly parade of accused people, Judge Monte Harris lost his patience when Jaekyu Yi launched into his sob story about being refused legal-aid funding.
>
> "Are you listening to me?" the Ontario Court judge asked sharply earlier this week. "Feb. 4 is your date for trial, whether you have a lawyer or not."
>
> Outside Courtroom 114 at Toronto's Old City Hall courthouse, Mr. Yi – who was charged with possession of 1.2 grams of marijuana – admitted he was not overly concerned.
>
> While he could not afford a private lawyer's retainer himself, Mr. Yi said he knew someone who could: "I'll just have to make my parents pay."

This is terrific. Makin establishes the time – "after a morning" – and mood – an "unruly parade of accused people." "Judge" tells us we're in a courtroom, and Makin prepares us for a confrontation between Judge Harris and Mr. Yi, whose suspicious "sob" story is causing the judge to lose his temper. Makin ends the first sentence by deftly introducing his theme – legal-aid funding.

After recording the judge's explosion – "Are you listening to me?" – Makin rushes off to get Mr. Yi's side of the story. He saves the punch line for the end, and the phrase "make my parents pay" sketches in Mr. Yi's character and his family relationships.

Having established one point of view on legal aid, Makin immediately introduces others:

"But for every Jaekyu Yi who comes up with a retainer, legal observers say, there is a far larger number who have been hit hard by the cut in legal aid.

"'It's just appalling,' said Judge Lynn King of the Ontario Court's Provincial Division. 'Ninety per cent of our clientele in family court are appearing unrepresented. These people are in crisis, but they often don't even know how to fill out forms.'"

The page-one story ends here with the notice: please see page 11. I flip to page 11, and I find that it evolves into a much longer, more complex debate that will lead to future stories, but it doesn't tell me much more than the first five paragraphs.

My second example comes from the back page of the first section under another awful headline: "A wet and windy cure for itchy feet." What is this, a homeopathic remedy? The story, by Betty Gibbs, is in a series of slice-of-life vignettes submitted by the public. I like these stories, so I start to read:

The dark depression of winter has settled over the city. Bloody January again!

We sat by the fire last fall and knew it was coming: we dreamed of warmth and sunshine and planned our escape. First we had to renew our passports. You know what they say about passport pictures: If you really look like that you probably aren't fit to travel. But they'd do. We weren't trying to win a beauty contest.

With photos in hand we headed to the passport office one wet and windy morning in November and, as instructed, we took a number. Number 64. The first number we heard called was nine. We had settled down for a long wait when we noticed a sign saying that passports now cost $60, cash or certified cheque. They've certainly gone up, and a quick check through purses and pockets indicated that a trip to the bank was necessary.

Rain pelted, wind whipped along the almost deserted streets as we made a quick dash to the downtown branch of our suburban bank. Number 38 was being called by the time we got back.

Gibbs is setting up one of those Chaplinesque encounters with bureaucracy I love to read about, but she makes me work too hard to get to the story. Where am I? Is it January or November? If it's November, why the big rush? Who is "we"? I assume from the context that the mystery person is her husband, but who knows? It would have been easy to say, "My husband, Don, and I. . . ." How old are they? If they are elderly or frail, then the storm becomes a greater peril. Why not use the passport photos to establish age and appearance?

Where is the passport office? An editor's note at the end of the story tells me Betty Gibbs lives in Victoria. Why not identify Victoria in the first sentence? Locate the office on a street. How far have Betty and her husband had to come? "Suburban" suggests some distance, and since this will be a story about running around in the rain trying to get their application forms signed, distance is important. Did they get cold? Wet feet?

Who? What? Where? When? Why? and *How?* These are my best friends, journalism's Fabulous Five Plus One. *Memorize them.* Count them out on your fingers. Tatoo them on your forearm. Think of them as a rock band, the Group of Six or the Six Dwarfs. By answering these questions as you write, you will not only give your story clarity and precision, but avoid clumsy phrases like "a quick search through purses and pockets." Had Gibbs given her husband a name, she could have written: "I checked my purse while Don rummaged in his pockets. Between us, we came up with $14.53."

It's a pity the editor didn't ask Gibbs to make these simple changes, since Gibbs solves many problems herself in the rest of her story. We meet Greg, the pharmacist who signs their forms, and Greg adds to the stress – his smoke alarm is going off. Gibbs knows how to use confrontation and dialogue – her husband needles her – and she expresses exasperation indirectly by piling incident on incident. It has the ingredients of a good story, and it's not her fault that the headline writer blows it by telegraphing the end – the Gibbs decide to stay home.

Journalism isn't the only model. How about: "In the beginning, God created the Heaven and the Earth"? Or the opening paragraph of *The Pilgrim's Progress*: "As I walked through the wilderness of this world, I lighted on a certain place where was a Den, and I laid me down in that place to sleep; and as I slept, I dreamed a dream. I dreamed, and behold, I saw a man clothed with rags, standing in a certain place, with his face from his own house, a book in his hand, and a great burden upon his back. I looked, and saw him open the book, and read therein; and, as he read, he wept, and trembled; and, not being able longer to contain, he brake out with a lamentable cry, saying, 'What shall I do?' "

John Bunyan identifies himself as the storyteller and uses a dream to signal to his readers that the events he is about to describe are not to be taken literally. His opening phrase, "as I walked," and the powerful forward thrust of his prose, put his narrative in motion before his pilgrim's progress begins. Bunyan enlists the reader's sympathy by describing the pilgrim's pitiful physical and emotional state, and engages our interest by asking a direct question.

Echoes of *The Pilgrim's Progress* are found everywhere in western literature, from the works of Albert Camus to the "I have a dream" speech of Martin Luther King. Even Lenin called one of his communist pamphlets "What Is to Be Done?" The danger of borrowing is cliché. The dream has been done to death, and I'm waiting for Disney to turn Christian's travails into an animated film, with saturation marketing of Slough of Despond coffee mugs.

Don't imitate. Adapt. *The Pilgrim's Progress* is the prototype for the twentieth-century American "road" book: some strung-out dude in deep shit hits the pavement and meets a whole lot of freaked-out folks before he makes it to the Celestial City, Los Angeles. Hunter S. Thompson's classic of Gonzo journalism, "Fear and Loathing in Las Vegas," owes a lot to Bunyan:

"We were somewhere around Barstow on the edge of the desert when the drugs began to take hold. I remember saying something like 'I feel a bit lightheaded; maybe you should drive . . .' And suddenly there was a terrible roar all around us and the sky was full of what looked like huge bats, all swooping and screeching and diving around the car, which was going about a hundred miles an hour with the top down to Las Vegas. And a voice was screaming: 'Holy Jesus! What are these goddamn animals?'"

And, as its title implies, "Fear and Loathing in Las Vegas" is a puritan morality tale.

Don't worry if your style is quiet and circumspect. A good lead can also be a slow pan, wide-angle shot. Here's how Truman

Capote opens his real-life thriller, *In Cold Blood* (Random House, 1965):

> The village of Holcomb stands on the high wheat plains of western Kansas, a lonesome area that other Kansans call "out there." Some seventy miles east of the Colorado border, the countryside, with its hard blue skies and desert-clear air, has an atmosphere that is rather more Far West than Middle West. The local accent is barbed with a prairie twang, a ranch-hand nasalness, and the men, many of them, wear narrow frontier trousers, Stetsons, and high-heeled boots with pointed toes. The land is flat, and the views are awesomely extensive; horses, herds of cattle, a white cluster of grain elevators rising as gracefully as Greek temples are visible long before a traveler reaches them.

Capote is telling us much more than a camera could. He identifies the village, locates it on a map, zooms in for a close-up of men in high-heeled boots, and overhears them talking. A combination of "hard blue skies," "desert-clear air," and "Far West" hints at a shoot-out, and he strikes an ominous chord with "lonesome" and "out there." Capote's drawling, loping style suits both the landscape and the story.

Writing the first paragraph forces you to solve several basic problems:

1. Are you going to write in the present tense, past tense, or use both? Capote begins in the present tense, then, after four paragraphs, tells the rest of his story in the past tense. Choose the tense that suits your anecdote, chapter, or story, but don't write: "As the sun broke through the clouds, I go out to the car. . . ."

I find the present tense works well in eyewitness stories and you-are-there documentary. Comedians use it all the time: "So I call my mother, and she says. . . ." Betty Gibbs's passport story would have been stronger written in the present tense: "We take a number, 64. The first number we hear called is nine. Rain pelts down, wind whips. . . ."

This is how I start *Grass Roots*, a documentary about rural life on the Canadian prairies:

"The knife makes a small cracking sound as it cuts through the vein and breaks the neck. The lamb grunts and makes frantic running motions with its trussed legs as the blood spurts out and runs down its side. Small, mangy black cats scuffle in from the dark corners of the barn and crouch in the straw in an expectant circle. Rolling its eye balefully upwards, breathing hard, the lamb raises and lowers its head. Close beside the lamb, the dog Ringo leans forward occasionally and tenderly licks the blood from the wound. 'Sheep,' says Gordon Taylor, 'take forever to die.'"

The present tense plunges the reader into the scene, and active verbs move the story ahead quickly. The constant present, however, makes it difficult to reflect, and a pell-mell pace eventually exhausts the reader. Hunter S. Thompson writes in the past tense, but his copious dialogue creates the illusion that events are unfolding before our eyes. A quote, such as Judge Harris's "Are you listening to me?" brings us into the present, although the events took place in the past. If you choose the past tense, try not to get bogged down in constructions like: "He wished he had thought of that. . . ."

Vary the pace of your story. Exciting events should be told in rapid, short sentences and graphic images. Exposition or reflection demands a quieter, more methodical pace. Pause. Look around. Even a short story should move at various speeds. A story that loses momentum, or plods along at a steady clop, clop, clop, bores the reader. It should bore you too. Listen to the rhythm of your sentences. A writer, like a symphony conductor, needs to orchestrate the trumpets with the violins.

2. Will you put yourself in your story as "I," or will you be unobtrusive and omniscient? Telling a story in the first person may seem simple and straightforward but, like the sorcerer's apprentice, "I" tends to run amok. A repetitive, omnipresent "I" may skew the focus of your story towards yourself, although your story may be about someone else. It restricts your point of view, and it can become irritating. The emphasis should not be on "I" but on what I am seeing.

A popular alternative is Capote's "I am a camera" approach, which substitutes the unobtrusive "eye" for "I." Norman Mailer sometimes chooses to objectify himself as "Mailer," a variation on the antiquated British practice of replacing "I" with "one," as in: "How good one feels to be back in one's own home." If you feel shy about "I," get it out of your story. I use "you" a lot in this book, but do it carefully. I don't like writers speaking for me, and if "you" really means "I," say so.

3. How do you organize your research? What do you leave out? This is a daunting task, especially when you have collected boxes full of papers and tapes, but if you have kept my story in mind, you have a good inkling of the relative importance of my material.

I file as I go, stuffing related material into folders labelled by subject, location, or source – people who lend me things want them back – and stack my files on the shelves and floor of my room. This messy method requires a lot of rummaging at first, but I soon learn where everything is, and less important material sifts to the bottom. A story grows, often in unexpected directions, and I am reluctant to impose too rigorous a system on it at the beginning. My research is, in effect, a compost heap. Use whatever method suits you, but remember you're a writer, not a librarian. Filing material alphabetically or chronologically, for instance, destroys its context; filing stuff you'll never use is a waste of time.

Discard *nothing* until your story is written or published. I invariably discover as I write that a piece of information I have ignored becomes critically important, and I have spent panicky hours searching for scraps of paper. If it's a magazine story, a fact checker will likely need to review your research and contact your sources. You have to produce that paper trail. You also need it in case there is controversy (see Chapter 10). I keep my research for a year or more after publication.

As you wade through paper or transcribe interviews, remember the imaginary reader peering over your shoulder asking: "What *is* all this stuff?" Readers are sceptical, and they have definite tastes: they love romance and biographies, they loathe statistics and government reports. If you feel lost, let your imaginary reader pull you back for a fresh perspective on your research.

It's always tempting to include material simply because it's *there*, like Mount Everest, and you've gone to a lot of trouble and expense to get it. Quantity, however, is not quality, and like any mountain climber, you have to hack a path to the top. Think of your story as a lifeline, a rope that runs from your opening paragraphs to the end. Push aside material that weighs you down, obstructs your path, or leads off on a tangent. Cutting hurts, but when in doubt, leave it out.

4. How do you choose? What *is* your story? A story evolves out of characters in conflict. What happens? Why? Who's there? What's it about? What do the antagonists have to say? How is it resolved?

Define points of conflict. Identify the people involved. Eliminate everyone else or reduce them to supporting roles. Narrow your cast to the most interesting people, and pit them against each other.

Isn't this ruthless? Yes. At this point a "person" becomes a "character." You may be creating a story out of living flesh, but, like a plastic surgeon, you shape that flesh to suit your model. Use only the strongest, most relevant parts of your interviews. Leave bodies on the cutting-room floor. If a story is crammed with too many peripheral characters, readers can't remember who's who. Choose a powerful running character who will appear throughout your story. Many journalists cast themselves in this role, turning their journey into their plot.

Establish your characters in the reader's imagination as soon as you introduce them. Remember, you know these people, but your readers have never met them. Use the whole first name, "Peter Stevens," the first time, then simply "Stevens," or if this is an intimate story, "Pete." There is no need to add Mr., Mrs., Ms. In place of the full name, two initials – "P. B. Stevens" – will do. One initial won't do. If Stevens is a doctor, introduce him as "Dr. P. B. Stevens" then drop the "Dr." Ignore all the LLDs, PhDs, OCs, and other things people tack onto their names. In the world of journalism, we are all equal.

Paint a brief, memorable portrait of this person. In *Cloak of Green* (Lorimer, 1995), an exposé of environmentalist politics, Canadian journalist Elaine Dewar describes her meeting with the organizer of the 1992 Rio Summit on the environment, Maurice Strong: "His brown suit was rumpled, his hair white and askew. He was nondescript, of average height, average weight, with a small moustache, but his hands were huge – big enough to pull hot iron into shapes. He coughed and coughed. He'd caught some form of pneumonia and had spent almost a month in bed back home in Colorado at the Baca Grande ranch. He spat right into a garbage pail."

I'll never forget that garbage pail. The best images are active – coughing, spitting – and Strong's hands symbolize his power. If you set the scene and place your characters in the spotlight, the reader will visualize your story. *Where* your encounter is taking place – a living room, train, hotel – is as important as *who* is there, *why*, and *how* they got there.

If your story involves a lot of people, it's even more essential to give each one a thumbnail portrait that sticks in the reader's mind. Train yourself to remember the colour of eyes and hair; observe clothing, jewellery, hands, teeth, skin, sounds, and smells. Capsulize personality by describing gestures or tone of voice. Walter Stewart's early book about Prime Minister Pierre Trudeau was aptly titled *Shrug*.

5. Where do you begin? Your story should have a logical progression, but it can begin anywhere. If your story is a memoir, you may want to begin in the present, go back to your youth, move into middle age, return to your childhood, then come back to the present. Or you can begin in the middle, as Ken Dryden does in *The Game* (see Chapter 6), with the freedom to move backwards and forwards.

Avoid the procrustean bed of chronology. It's easy to switch time and place by starting a new chapter. However, if you jump, have a good reason. Leave out whole decades, but if one thing doesn't lead to another, the reader will get lost. Think of Hansel and Gretel and the breadcrumbs. At the same time, a story that is linear, one-dimensional, and predictable will not be very interesting. When I am writing complex stories, I think of myself as a weaver working threads into a tapestry.

Remember the arc: exposition, complication, climax, resolution. Tell the reader where you expect to be going, but if you blurt everything out on the first page, the rest will be anticlimactic. Save your best stuff, but don't keep it for the end. Your reader will lose interest, and newspaper editors cut stories from the bottom. Imagine your readers as a pack of wolves. Throw them enough meat to keep them on your trail, hungry for more. If they are still hungry at the end, you're alive! I keep up my sleeve a device called a *kicker*, an image or quote that ends my story with a bang, or boots it ahead into the next chapter.

FURTHER READING

Truman Capote, *In Cold Blood*, Random House, 1965. A perfect story, often mistaken for fiction, and still controversial.

Northrop Frye, *Anatomy of Criticism*, Princeton University Press, 1957. Everything you need to know about symbols, myths, and genres. Scholarly, but it more than repays the effort.

William Shakespeare, *King Lear, Hamlet, Macbeth, Richard III*. Many of Shakespeare's greatest plays were based on true stories. His genius was in the telling.

Hunter S. Thompson, *Fear and Loathing in Las Vegas and Other American Stories*, Modern Library, 1996. This edition includes Thompson's jacket notes for the first edition, an illuminating description of how the story grew out of an assignment for *Sports Illustrated* magazine. See also Thompson's sequel, "Fear and Loathing on the Campaign Trail, '72."

CHAPTER 4

Writing the Story: Plain Speech, Please

There is a popular misconception that good narrative prose is "literary" or "lyrical." Some good prose is lyrical; good prose can also be colloquial, sinewy, lucid and well-crafted, and don't sneeze at workmanlike. I shun pretentious phrases like "creative documentary" or "literary non-fiction," and I avoid stories by writers who constantly nudge me in the ribs saying: "Look Ma, I'm writing!" I mistrust anything labelled "experimental."

Your literary model is journalism. A true story is not an end in itself. It's a way of perceiving reality. If you stand in front of your window, or fog it up, you obscure your story. Be transparent. Use short paragraphs, simple sentences, and plain, descriptive words. Tell your story in the words you normally speak and hear around you. Spit it out.

Sound simple? I wish. When you begin to write, you will probably be horrified by what comes out on the page: bad grammar, clumsy circumlocutions, buzzwords, pompous phrases, limping adverbs, sentences that clang like a car dragging its muffler. Erase, and try again. Your word bank is full of sludge: phrases from books you were taught in school, stories you've read in newspapers, talk you hear on radio and television, scraps of dialogue from B movies.

You haven't been listening to your own voice, and in the deafening chatter of the mass media, it takes a while to find it. Erase, and try again. I call this "burning the carbon out of the engine." Keep the mechanics in mind:

Reject debased coinage, words and phrases so worn out by overuse they have no meaning: patriarchy, cutting edge, Generation X, world class. If a phrase strikes you as cute, and everybody's using it, kill it. It will likely die a natural death before your story is written, and if not, it should. Even the most prestigious publications are full of badly written non-stories.

Respect the strength, vitality, and history of the English language. Old English words have survived more than two thousand years – "word" is a good example – because they are precise and descriptive. Anglo-Saxon writers called a personal narrative a "wordhord," a mask was a "grimhelm," and the phrase "under cover of night" began as "nihthelm." We can see the legacy of Old English in contemporary words such as wetland, software, Web site, thinktank, and bafflegab.

These words are sensuous and compressed, and they have the crisp, satisfying sound of words being spoken. I love the image of a tank full of fishy intellectuals, or a shifty-eyed writer hunched over his pile of metaphors. Look through an Anglo-Saxon dictionary, and try reading the Old English epic poem, *Beowulf*, in the original, aloud. Words that look incomprehensible may sound familiar, and *Beowulf* is as good an example as I can suggest of character, conflict, and story.

Get rid of gorp. Gorp is doodads and thingamajigs, those sloppy, decorative, redundant words and phrases that clutter up your prose. Strip down to nouns and verbs. This sentence is loaded with gorp: "On a warm, foggy morning in late September, I woke up late, feeling a little vague after a party I don't quite remember, and after putting on my only clean shirt, the one with red stripes, I ventured cautiously out into the mist to the local convenience store to buy something for my searing headache."

The writer slows the pace by backing in with a prepositional phrase. The singsong rhythm is soporific. What's important? Is it the fog? Headache? Party? Why do we need to know the shirt has red stripes? The phrase "a little vague" is vague, and so is "I don't quite remember." The verb "ventured" is weak, and adding "cautiously" doesn't make it stronger. "Mist" is mentioned again, to no apparent purpose. The store has no name, and "something for my searing headache" is an awkward way of saying "pain-killer." If he staggers to Becker's to buy Tylenol, we know he's feeling hungover.

Ask yourself: Do I need this word? Why? Is there a stronger way of writing the sentence? Watch out for "was," as in: "I was in the middle of the crosswalk when I was hit by a kid on a mountain bike." This is passive and dull. Turn it around: "A kid on a mountain bike knocked me down in the middle of the crosswalk." Writers fall into the common trap of starting sentences with "There was . . ." as in "There was a ship in the harbour." Why not say: "A sailboat bobbed at anchor in the harbour"?

Find a way to avoid similes: "He looked like a wrestler." What does a wrestler look like? Metaphors are more effective. In her autobiography, *Growing Pains* (Clarke, Irwin, 1946) artist Emily Carr describes an aristocratic friend this way:

"Mildred had been born condensed. Space alarmed her. She was like a hot loaf that had been put immediately into too small a bread-box and got misshapen by cramping. She was unaware of being cramped, because she was unconscious of any humans except those of her own class. The outer crowd propped her, but she was unaware of them. Away from crowds, Mildred flopped."

Similes and metaphors add colour and texture to your story, but larding on colour without form or purpose creates a mess of daubs and splatters. Here is a less successful sample from *Growing Pains*:

> It was wild lily time. We went through our garden, our cow-yard and pasture, and came to our wild lily field. Here we stood a little, quietly looking. Millions upon millions of white lilies were spangled over the green field. Every lily's brown eye looked down into the earth but her petals rolled back over her head and pointed at the pine-tree tops and the sky. No one could make words to tell how fresh and sweet they smelled. The perfume was delicate yet had such power its memory clung through the rest of your life and could carry you back any time to the old lily field, even after the field had become city and there were no more lilies in it – just houses and houses. Yes, even then your nose could ride on the smell and come galloping back to the lily field.

Carr takes a risk changing lilies into women. Then, having established herself standing in the field, she abruptly changes "we" into "you" and zooms from the past to the present. Carr fails to describe how the lilies smelled, and the image of the galloping nose is ludicrous.

Don't strip so much fat from your prose it becomes pale and anorexic. A "punk" kid on a mountain bike would add emotion and detail to your encounter, and "a blue mist shrouded the hills" is more effective than "mist shrouded the hills." Always try to use words that engage the reader's senses: sight, sound, touch, taste, and smell. In *Doing Battle* (Little, Brown, 1996), Paul Fussell conjures up his boyhood with this passage: "What boy can forget the taste of tennis-racket strings or violin-bow resin, or the tar used for road repairs? Wool tastes different from cotton, and both from paper, and paper from cardboard; licking wood is nothing like licking a tennis ball, and the rubber strings inside a golf ball taste entirely different from rubber bands."

The most evocative words create visceral or kinesthetic images that provoke a physical response in the reader, a wince of pain, a twinge of nausea, a gut reaction. A classic example is this short poem by Margaret Atwood:

you fit into me
like a hook into an eye

a fish hook
an open eye

Look for images with symbolic resonance: Proust's madeleine, the hyacinths in T. S. Eliot's *The Waste Land*, Albert Camus's Algerian desert. When I visited Indian reserves, I noticed that the resident white people, nurses, teachers, storekeepers, lived together in compounds of white-painted buildings; the Indians lived in the bush in log cabins or in houses painted earthy colours. There was my story, in one image. All writers rely on images associated with the four elements: earth, air, fire, and water.

Respect the rules. Stories are written in certain ways because they work. Write in sentences, not clumps of words, and vary the length of your paragraphs and sentences. Begin a new paragraph when you introduce a new thought or personality. Resist overdosing on CAPITAL LETTERS, **bold face**, or weird punctuation . . .!!!! Understand the words you are using: "flounder" is not the same as "founder," and "exploitive" is simpler than "exploitative." There is no need to create new words. A psychologist once told me about a client who "catastrophized" her situation, and I read about troubled people who "obsess" about their problems or "impact" others.

I have to translate this stuff into English. Yes, I do it myself, so I don't have to say: "I, myself."

Use a good dictionary. A thesaurus will help you expand your vocabulary, but never use bloated, obscure words to impress people unless you're a windbag. A style guide may make things easier (but not one intended for scholars writing academic papers) and the writers' bible, Fowler's *Modern English Usage*, should always be at hand.

HE SAID, SHE SAID

I like quotes because my interviews can do the work. A good quote is an observation or anecdote told in a lively way that reveals personality and moves the story along. Quote entire sentences. Don't chop interviews into liver and try to mash the bits together. "Historians," I notice, "seem to be particularly prone" to this "atrocity." Write: "Historians," I notice, "seem to be particularly prone to this atrocity."

Vary your presentation: "I said, 'Historians seem to be particularly prone to this atrocity.'" Avoid weaker substitutions: I recalled, I thought, I supposed. If you can, get rid of "he said, she said." In her book, *The Perfection of Hope* (Macfarlane Walter & Ross, 1997), Elizabeth Simpson effectively eliminates quotation marks by writing the quotes in italics. If you use quotation marks, highlight the quote by beginning a new paragraph, and splice quotes together to give the illusion people are talking to each other. Borrow from fiction. Borrow from radio.

In my three years as a radio producer with the Canadian Broadcasting Corporation, I commissioned a lot of interviews, and I spliced a lot of tape. I spliced the tape by hand, with a razor blade, on a steel block, and I put it all together with sticky tape.

It was a great education: one slip and I'd lose a word, or a pause. Listen. Convey the rhythm and cadence of this person's speech, as well as their gropings and idiosyncratic expressions. Can your reader follow? It may be necessary to tidy garbled sentences or bridge gaps, but don't rewrite the interview to conform to your own, or your editor's, way of speaking. Don't put bridge words in [square brackets] unless you can do so unobtrusively or the words are potentially controversial. Most people won't remember exactly what they said, and will be pleased to appear articulate.

In most cases, you have no obligation to reproduce sentences exactly as they are spoken. You will find yourself beginning with a quote from the middle or end of your interview, condensing thoughts, and rearranging the order of sentences. Eliminate the "you know"s, "like"s, and "ummm"s unless they reveal character or relate to your theme. Shape your material according to your story. Quotes should be clear and comprehensible, yet your reader may need to get the impression that English is this person's second language, or that they have difficulty speaking. Capture rhythms and accents, as Truman Capote does so well. People in Saskatchewan, for instance, tend to drop their gs, and in rural southern Ontario, the soft, ambiguous phrase "Oh, yeah," used everywhere else in Canada to convey scepticism, approval, curiosity, and cynicism, becomes a harsh, aggressive oink: "Oiya, oiya, oiya!"

Use a quote to highlight character, introduce a new voice, or break up your narrative. Quotes should add drama and authenticity to your story. Don't quote anything you can say better yourself. It's almost always a bad idea to begin a story with a quote: Who is this person? Why are they saying this? Quotes are more effective once the speaker's role in the story is clear and the reader's expectations are aroused.

A quote also helps you change "point of view." Take a look at a screenplay. It will be studded with the letters "POV," the writer's instructions to the director to shoot the scene from a particular Point Of View. Changing POV can work as effectively for narrative. If you feel your story bogging down, maybe it's time to start a new paragraph or chapter from a fresh angle. Capote, for instance, tells the first part of *In Cold Blood* POV victims, the middle chapters POV murderers, and the last section POV detectives.

If you are writing in the first person, you might give the reader a glimpse of what you look like to someone else. How old are you? What are you wearing? E. B. White, Norman Mailer, Paul Theroux, and Hunter S. Thompson are always looking at their reflections or being watched by imaginary watch-birds. A self-reflective POV is no less egocentric, but it helps break up the monotonous "I" and "me" and establishes ironic distance.

Another cinematic trick is to tell your story in scenes or episodes. These can be as short as a sentence or as long as a chapter. We accept quick cuts in film and video, so if your story has momentum, most readers will make the jump. Some editors still want to drag the reader by the nose through laborious "transitions" loaded with "but," "however," and "nevertheless." I resist. If necessary, leaving a double white space on your page should do the job. I also resist "foreshadowing," dropping hints about what is to come, as in: "little did she know that in ten years. . . ."

As you wrestle with these problems and the words begin to flow more easily, you will find yourself listening to your "voice." Your storytelling voice will likely bear no resemblance to the voice you use in conversation, and may vary from story to story, but it should be uniquely and unmistakably yours. Farley Mowat, June Callwood, and Mordecai Richler have distinct, recognizable voices; so do most newspaper and magazine columnists.

Your voice will grab your readers' attention, or turn them off, and it will establish the tone of your story. There is a difference, for instance, between wit and sarcasm, introspection and self-pity, rage and bombast. Your voice may infuriate as many people as it charms, but at least you have their attention. The trick is not to write in a boring drone, or irritate people to the point where they ignore you.

Read your work aloud, at least under your breath. If your tongue trips and stumbles, something is wrong. Ask yourself: Does this ring true? Why not? You may be trying to write the way you think you should, not the way you know how. Don't deliberately imitate other writers; their influence is already pervasive. Canadian literature, for instance, has been constipated by what I call the Upper Canadian voice, a fastidious, aggrieved tone adopted by members of the English gentry who wrote stories about the tribulations of life in the colonies. Read Susanna Moodie's *Roughing It in the Bush* (McClelland & Stewart, 1962), but don't copy it.

Readers are as interested in you, the teller, as they are in your story. Your subject matter, tone of voice, choice of language, images, and rhythm of speech all reveal your personality, or the persona you develop to write the story. Your persona isn't you, although readers may think it is. Readers are always amazed to discover that a writer famous for folksy, crackerbarrel tales has the charm of a cobra, or that a poison-pen columnist is timid and tongue-tied.

Storytellers have always worn costumes, and identified ourselves with others in our craft. We are familiar with the blind poet, the jester in cap and bells, the guitar-strumming troubadour, the Angry Young Man, and the Intrepid Explorer. (It was, after all, an American journalist, H. B. Stanley, who tracked down the British missionary David Livingstone in the depths of the African jungle and asked, as any good journalist would, "Dr. Livingstone, I presume?")

Where do you fit? The persona of the Bitch Goddess has done well for feminist writers, and Robert Bly has countered with the Iron Man. As we see in the following chapters, your persona will evolve from the literary tradition you choose.

FURTHER READING

T. S. Eliot, *The Complete Poems and Plays*, Harcourt Brace, New York. For sensuous imagery, symbolism, and the use of voices, Eliot is hard to beat.

William Strunk, Jr., *The Elements of Style*, with an introduction and a chapter on writing by E. B. White. An old book, slightly out of date, but smart, short, and funny.

William Zinsser, *On Writing Well*, Fifth Edition, HarperPerennial (paper). Basic, breezy, the best of the recent American how-to books. Zinsser has decades of experience as a true-story writer, an editor, and a teacher of writing.

CHAPTER 5

The Journal

Literature in Canada began with the journals kept by the priests and explorers who established the empire of New France in the first half of the seventeenth century. The journal, a term derived from *jour*, the French word for day, was then emerging as a literary form, a means not only of recording daily events, but of communicating information, transactions, and opinions to distant governors, bureaucrats, and patrons. In English, the journal became associated with journey, as a record of travel; a journeyman, for instance, was an artisan who travelled from village to village to ply his trade. Journalism, therefore, is a craft defined by adventure, observation, and record-keeping. The journal was ideally suited to the discovery of a "new" world, where everything seemed so fabulous to European eyes that merely describing everyday life was enough to astonish the reader.

"It was here that I saw Savages for the first time," Father Paul LeJeune wrote to his superior in France from Tadoussac, Quebec, in April 1632. "It seemed to me that I was looking at those maskers who run about France in Carnival time. There were some whose noses were painted blue, the eyes, eyebrows, and cheeks painted black, and the rest of the face red; and these colours are bright and shining like those of our masks; others had black, red, and blue stripes drawn from the ears to the mouth."

LeJeune goes on to sketch in detail the Montagnards' clothing and manners, and later describes, with horror and disgust, their practice of torturing and eating their enemies. LeJeune, a cranky Roman Catholic priest on a wilderness mission to harvest souls among the barbarians, makes no pretence of being objective – the Jesuit *Relations* reveal as much about the priests' own personalities as the circumstances in which they found themselves.

"A little place like their cabins is easily heated by a good fire, which sometimes roasted and broiled me on all sides," LeJeune complained about his first winter among the Indians.

> You cannot move to right or left, for the Savages, your neigh-bours, are at your elbows; you cannot withdraw to the rear, for you encounter the wall of snow, or the bark of the cabin which shuts you in. Had I stretched myself out, my legs would have been halfway in the fire; to roll myself up in a ball, and crouch down that way, was a position I could not retain as long as they could; my clothes were all scorched and burned. But as to the smoke, I confess to you that it is martyrdom. It almost killed me, and made me weep continually, although I had neither grief nor sadness in my heart. It sometimes caused us to place our mouths against the earth in order to breathe; as it were to eat the earth, so as not to eat the smoke.

By describing the Montagnards' winter dwelling through the lens of his own discomfort, LeJeune brings our senses and emotions into play. We can feel heat and cold, cramped limbs, smarting eyes, claustrophobia and suffocation. LeJeune casts himself in a heroic role as martyr – self-pity is a characteristic common to journal keepers – and his squabbles with the shaman who got him into this miserable mess, the Sorcerer, give his *relation* the drama and conflict of a wartime despatch from the front.

Martyrdom had become a literary *cause célèbre* with the publication in 1563 of *Actes and Monuments of These Latter Perilous Days*, commonly called *The Book of Martyrs*, by an English Protestant polemicist, John Foxe. Foxe describes torture, suffering, and violent death in such relentless, bloody detail, and with such emotional fervour, he could be accused of writing sado-masochistic pornography. Foxe deflects this criticism, however, by insisting that he is merely relating the facts, and bolsters the authenticity of his stories with eyewitness reports.

Foxe's motives were religious, but he had discovered the literary potential of true crime: Protestants read *The Book of Martyrs* as avidly as the Bible. So did Catholics, it appears. Foxe's influence is seen in this 1678 memoir by Christophe Regnaut, a shoemaker who had been a lay volunteer with the Jesuit mission at Ste. Marie near Lake Huron in 1649. It is such a good example of reportage I quote it in full:

A Veritable Account of the Martyrdom and Blessed Death of Father Jean de Brébeuf and of Father Gabriel L'Alemant, in New France, in the Country of the Hurons, by the Iroquois, Enemies of the Faith.

Father Jean de Brébeuf and Father Gabriel L'Alemant had set out from our cabin to go to a small village, called St. Ignace, distant from our cabin about a short quarter of a league, to instruct the Savages and the new Christians of that Village. It was on the 16th day of March, in the morning, that we perceived a great fire at the place to which these two good fathers had gone. This fire made us very uneasy; we did not know whether it were enemies, or if the fire had caught in some of the huts of the village.

The Reverend Father Paul Ragueneau, our Superior, immediately resolved to send someone to learn what might be the cause. But no sooner had we formed the design of going there to see, than we perceived several savages on the road, coming straight towards us. We all thought it was the Iroquois who were coming to attack us; but having considered them more closely, we perceived that they were Hurons who were fleeing from the fight, and who had escaped from the combat. These poor savages caused great pity in us. They were all covered with wounds. One had his head fractured; another his arm broken; another had an arrow in his eye; another had his hand cut off by a blow from a hatchet. In fine, the day was passed in receiving into our cabins all these poor wounded people, and in looking with compassion toward the fire, and the place where were those two good Fathers. We saw the fire and the barbarians, but we could not see anything of the Fathers.

This is what these savages told us of the taking of the Village of St. Ignace, and about Fathers Jean de Brébeuf and Gabriel L'Alemant:

"The Iroquois came, to the number of twelve hundred men, took our village, and seized Father Brébeuf and his companion, and set fire to all the huts. They proceeded to vent their rage on these two Fathers, for they took them both and stripped them entirely naked, and fastened each to a post. They tied both of their hands together. They tore the nails from the fingers. They beat them with a shower of blows from cudgels, on the shoulders, the loins, the belly, the legs and the face – there being no part of their body which did not endure this torment."

The savages told us further, that, although Father de Brébeuf was overwhelmed under the weight of these blows, he did not cease continually to speak of God, and to encourage all the new Christians who were captives like himself to suffer well, that they might die well, in order to go in company with him to Paradise. While the good Father was thus encouraging these good people, a wretched Huron renegade – who had remained a captive with the Iroquois, and whom Father de Brébeuf had formerly instructed and baptized – hearing him speak of Paradise and Holy Baptism, was irritated, and said to him, "Echon," that is Father de Brébeuf's name in Huron, "thou sayest that Baptism and the sufferings of this life lead straight to Paradise; thou wilt go soon, for I am going to baptize thee, and to make thee suffer well, in order to go the sooner to Paradise."

The barbarian, having said that, took a kettle full of boiling water, which he poured over his body three different times, in derision of Holy baptism. And, each time that he baptized him in this manner, the barbarian said to him, with bitter sarcasm, "Go to Heaven, for thou art well baptized."

After that, they made him suffer several other torments. The first was to make hatchets red-hot, and to apply them to the loins and under the armpits. They made a collar of these red-hot hatchets, and put it on the neck of this good Father. This is the fashion in which I have seen the collar made for other prisoners: They make six hatchets red-hot, take a large withe of green wood, pass the six hatchets over the large end of the withe, take the two ends together, and then put it over the neck of the sufferer. I have seen no torment which moved me more to compassion than that. For you see a man, bound naked to a post, who, having this collar on his neck, cannot tell what posture to take. For, if he lean forward, those above his shoulders weigh the more on him; if he lean back, those on his stomach make him suffer the same torment; if he keep erect, without leaning to one side or the other, the burning hatchets, applied equally on both sides, give him a double torture.

After that they put on him a belt of bark, full of pitch and resin, and set fire to it, which roasted him whole body. During all these torments, Father de Brébeuf endured like a rock, insensible to fire and flames, which astonished all the bloodthirsty wretches who tormented him. His zeal was so great that he preached continually to these infidels, to try to convert them. His executioners were enraged against him for constantly speaking to them of God and of their conversion. To prevent him from speaking more, they cut off his tongue, and both his upper and lower lips. After that, they set themselves to strip the flesh from his legs, thighs and arms, to the very bone; and then put it to roast before his eyes, in order to eat it.

While they tormented him in this manner, those wretches derided him, saying, "Thou seest plainly that we treat thee as a friend, since we shall be the cause of thy Eternal happiness; thank us, then, for these good offices which we render thee – for, the more thou shalt suffer, the more will thy God reward thee."

Those butchers, seeing that the good Father began to grow weak, made him sit down on the ground; and one of them, taking a knife, cut off the skin covering his skull. Another one of those barbarians, seeing that the good Father would soon die, made an opening in the upper part of his chest, and tore out his heart, which he roasted and ate. Others came to drink his blood, still warm, which they drank with both hands – saying that Father de Brébeuf had been very courageous to endure so much pain as they had given him, and that, by drinking his blood, they would become courageous like him.

This is what we learned of the Martyrdom and blessed death of Father Jean de Brébeuf, by several Christian savages worthy of belief, who had been constantly present from the time the good Father was taken until his death. These good Christians were prisoners to the Iroquois, who were taking them into their country to be put to death. But our good God granted them the favour of enabling them to escape by the way; and they came to us to recount all that I have set down in writing.

Father de Brébeuf was captured on the 16th day of March, in the morning, with Father L'Alemant, in the year 1649. Father de Brébeuf died the same day as his capture, about 4 o'clock in the afternoon. Those barbarians threw the remains of his body into the fire; but the fat which still remained on his body extinguished the fire, and he was not consumed.

I do not doubt that all I have just related is true, and I would seal it in my blood; for I have seen the same treatment given to Iroquois prisoners whom the Huron savages have taken in war, with the exception of the boiling water, which I have not seen poured on anyone.

I am about to describe to you truly what I saw of the Martyrdom and of the Blessed Deaths of Father Jean de Brébeuf and of Father Gabriel L'Alemant. On the next morning, when we had assurance of the departure of the enemy, we went to the spot to seek for the remains of their bodies, to the place where their lives had been taken. We found them both, but a little apart from each other. They were brought to our cabin, and laid uncovered upon the bark of trees – where I examined them at leisure, for more than two hours, to see if what the savages had told us of their martyrdom and death were true.

I examined first the Body of Father de Brébeuf, which was pitiful to see, as well as that of Father L'Alemant. Father de Brébeuf had his legs, thighs and arms stripped of flesh to the very bone; I saw and touched a large number of great blisters, which he had on several places on his body, from the boiling water which these barbarians had poured over him in mockery of Holy Baptism. I saw and touched the wound from a belt of bark, full of pitch and resin, which roasted him whole body. I saw and touched the marks of burns from the collar of hatchets placed on his shoulders and stomach. I saw and touched his two lips, which they had cut off because he spoke constantly of God while they made him suffer.

I saw and touched all parts of his body, which had received more than two hundred blows from a stick; I saw and touched the top of his scalped head: I saw and touched the opening which these barbarians had made to tear out his heart. In fine, I saw and touched all the wounds of his body, as the savages had told and declared to us: we buried these precious Relics on Sunday, the 21st day of March, 1649, with much Consolation.

I had the happiness of carrying them to the grave, and of burying them with those of Father Gabriel L'Alemant. When we left the country of the Hurons, we raised both bodies out of the ground, and set them to boil in strong lye. All the bones were well-scraped and the care of drying them was given to me. I put them every day into a little oven which we had, made of clay, after having heated it slightly, and when in a state to be packed, they were separately enveloped in silk stuff. Then they were put into two small chests, and we brought them to Quebec, where they are held in great veneration.

It is not a Doctor of the Sorbonne who has composed this, as you may easily see; it is a relic from the Iroquois, and a person who has lived more than thought – who is, and ever shall be, Sir, Your Very Humble and very obedient servant, Christophe Regnaut.

Like John Foxe, Regnaut meticulously records eyewitness accounts, but he does not accept them at face value. He peppers his witnesses with questions, and exacts from them all possible details. He is not content until he has cross-checked his witnesses' accounts with other sources, and visited the site to see for himself. More than that, Regnaut confirms his visual and hearsay evidence by *touching* and *smelling* the victims' bodies, then carefully describes their disposal.

Regnaut's account is precise, dramatic, brimming with information and full of activity. He begins by establishing time, location, suspense, and the central image of his story, fire. The breathless arrival of the fleeing Hurons sets the stage for their account of the confrontation between Brébeuf and his Iroquois tormentor, and Regnaut heightens the immediacy by quoting dialogue. The climax of the story, Brébeuf's murder, is told in simple, powerful words – cudgels, belly, knife, skull, blood – that arouse in the reader an empathetic physical response.

To this point, Regnaut has played the role of listener. Once Brébeuf is dead, however, Regnaut enters the action himself as undertaker, detective, witness, guardian, and recorder (he was a shoemaker, not a priest). The mood becomes quiet and elegiac; the repetition of "I saw and touched" is almost a chant. Regnaut brings his story to a close with a fire image – the drying of the bones – that is a satisfying progression from his earlier evocations of fire and ashes. His wry, self-deprecatory sign-off gives a glimpse of his practical, self-assured personality, and he doesn't fail to leave the reader with a teasing mystery – why has he paid such scant attention to Father L'Alemant?

Regnaut's account may in fact be full of errors and omissions, but he has presented himself as such an authoritative witness that he is completely convincing. He is saying: "This is true. I was there, and I've got the bones to prove it." A true story has to be verifiable. People, dates, and places must be identified, the details correct, the dialogue authentic, and the events genuine.

Most writers ignore these basic principles. As a manuscript editor and juror in literary competitions, I have read countless stories told by invisible narrators about nameless people involved in unresolved relationships in unidentified locations at no point in time. They make me scream with exasperation.

Journalism is precise and verifiable because the first North American explorers could not afford to make mistakes: faulty information jeopardized the lives of everyone following in their paths. The journals of Pierre-Esprit Radisson, La Vérendrye, Alexander Henry "The Younger," and, in particular, Samuel Hearne, defined Canadian literature as a narrative concerned with landscape, survival, cultural clash, and moral struggle.

Their journals, together with the Jesuit *Relations*, contain the seeds of all the literary forms we use today: travel and adventure, reportage, diary, memoir, confessional, true crime, sermon, history, biography, fiction, even poetry. E. J. Pratt drew on the *Relations* for his epic poem "Brébeuf and his Brethren," a staple of grade-school English classes until our self-perception became less one-sided, and more recently, novelist Brian Moore creatively reworked the Jesuits' stories in *Black Robe*. Rudy Wiebe, a scholar of exploration literature, bases his novels entirely on real people and events, and two of his best, *The Temptations of Big Bear* and *A Discovery of Strangers*, feature violent confrontations between white soldiers and aboriginal people. Guy Vanderhaeghe picked up the theme of native/white culture clash in his 1995 historical novel, *An Englishman's Boy*, and the enormous literature around Louis

Riel, including an opera, indicates that, at least in western Canada, the theme of martyrdom has not lost its grip on our imaginations.

In *Survival*, her 1972 thematic guide to Canadian literature, Margaret Atwood doesn't refer specifically to the explorers' journals, but she describes their influence:

> The central symbol for Canada is undoubtedly Survival, *la Survivance*. It is a multi-faceted and adaptable idea. For early explorers and settlers, it meant bare survival in the face of "hostile" elements and/or natives; carving out a place and a way of keeping alive. But the word can also suggest survival of a crisis or disaster, like a hurricane or a wreck; what you might call "grim" survival as opposed to "bare" survival.
>
> Our stories are likely to be tales not of those who made it but of those who made it back, from the awful experience – the North, the snowstorm, the sinking ship – that killed everyone else.

We are a culture of Ancient Mariners because only those explorers who made it back published their journals; those who didn't, among them Sir John Franklin, left no record. Our central myth, which Atwood describes as one of death, disaster, and victimization, has also been shaped by the fact that men like Radisson and Hearne didn't merely observe tragic or murderous events, they participated. When Radisson spent the winter of 1659 among the Huron near Lake Superior, he nearly starved to death. Here, in part, is his account:

> Every one cryes out for hungar; the women become baren, and drie like Wood. You men must eate the cord, being you have no more strength to make use of the bow, children, you must die. In the morning the husband looks uppon his

wife, the Brother his sister, the cozen the cozen that weare for the most part found deade. They languish with cryes and hideous noise that it was able to make the haire starre on the heads that have any apprehension. Good God have mercy on so many poore innocent people, and of us that acknowledge thee, that having offended thee punishes us. But wee are not free of that cruell Executioner.

The two first weeke we did eate our doggs. As we went back uppon our stepps for to gett anything to fill our bellyes, we weare glad to gett the boans and carcasses of the beasts that we killed; and happy was he that could gett what the other did throw away after it had been boyled three or fowre times to gett the substance out of it. We contrived to another plott, to reduce to powder those boanes, the rest of Crows and doggs, and boyled them againe and gave more froth than before. In the next place, the skins that weare reserved to make us shooes, cloath, and stokins, yea, most of the skins of our Cottages, the castors' skins, where the children beshit them above a hundred times, We burned the haire on the Coals. The rest goes downe throats eating heartily these things most abhorred. We went so eagerly to it that our gumms did bleede like one newly wounded. Finaly we became the very Images of death.

It is not Radisson's experience of starvation in itself that gives this passage its strength and authenticity, it's his ability to describe this experience in powerful images and to express frankly his feelings of horror and revulsion. Death and suffering were commonplace topics for writers of the early seventeenth century, Shakespeare among them, but the characteristic that stands out in early Canadian narrative is the writers' *empathy* for the sufferer.

"The shrieks and groans of the poor expiring wretches were truly dreadful," Samuel Hearne writes about the massacre of a camp of Esquimaux by the Indians with whom he was travelling in the summer of 1771.

My horror was much increased at seeing a young girl, seemingly about eighteen years of age, killed so near me, that when the first spear was stuck into her side she fell down at my feet, and twisted around my legs, so that it was with difficulty that I could disengage myself from her dying grasps.

As two Indian men pursued this unfortunate victim, I solicited very hard for her life; but the murderers made no reply till they had stuck both their spears through her body, and transfixed her to the ground. They then looked me sternly in the face, and began to ridicule me, by asking if I wanted an Esquimaux wife; and paid not the smallest regard to the shrieks and agony of the poor wretch, who was twining round their spears like an eel! Indeed, after receiving much abusive language from them on the occasion, I was at length obliged to desire that they would be more expeditious in dispatching their victim out of her misery, otherwise I should be obliged, out of pity, to assist in the friendly office of putting an end to the existence of a fellow creature who was so cruelly wounded. On this request being made, one of the Indians hastily drew his spear from the place where it was first lodged, and pierced it through her breast near the heart.

My situation and the terror of my mind at beholding his butchery cannot be easily conceived, much less described; though I summed up all the fortitude I was master of on the occasion, it was with difficulty that I could refrain from tears; and I am confident that my features must have feelingly expressed how sincerely I was affected at the barbarous scene

I then witnessed; even at this hour I cannot reflect on the transactions of that horrid day without shedding tears.

Hearne was an impressionable young man of twenty-six when he crossed the Barren Lands to the mouth of the Coppermine River on the Arctic Ocean, but, as this passage indicates, he did not write his *Journey from Prince of Wales's Fort in Hudson's Bay to the Northern Ocean* until twenty years later, after he had left the service of the Hudson's Bay Company and retired to England. His journal shows the influence of Jean-Jacques Rousseau's romantic ideas about "nature" and the "noble savage" – Hearne was shocked by the Indians' cruelty because he had for them otherwise the greatest admiration and respect – and his tearful remembrance of things past reflects the nostalgic *sensibilité* of Rousseau's *Confessions*.

Hearne, however, was no neurasthenic narcissist living in a dream world; he was a sailor and a trader, courageous, hard-headed, politically astute, an intelligent observer and an excellent judge of character. Hearne's "savages" were real, and dangerous: his awareness of the risk to his own life heightens the emotional tension of his confrontation over the dying girl. Like Radisson and the Jesuits, Hearne was in an ambivalent position, an outsider trapped in an indigenous war he could neither influence nor understand. He was, moreover, entirely dependent on the hospitality of his Indian hosts, especially the women, who did most of the work and provided comforts. Hearne's tender concern for the health and well-being of the native women, extraordinary in its time, was, under the circumstances, a matter of common sense and self-preservation.

By examining the literary baggage we carry around, we can see why writers adopt certain attitudes and points of view. In the seventeenth-century American colonies, English Puritans burned witches; in Canada, Iroquois sorcerers burned Jesuits. Explorers like Radisson and Hearne made it back because they adopted the sorcerers' point of view – even Christophe Regnaut gives the Iroquois due respect. Not until Betty Friedan published *The Feminine Mystique* in 1963 did an American journalist side with the witches.

If the Canadian tradition derives from the isolated, anxious explorer caught between a rock and a rapid, American narrative has been shaped by puritan fundamentalism and military conquest. The Canadian tradition is rooted in ambivalence – the Indians, French, and English are still going at it – while the Americans are stuck with the stereotype of the Great White Hunter. The once-dominant British narrative voice is becoming faint and unintelligible to North American ears.

One tradition is not better, or more creative, than another. Both derive from moral as well as physical conflict, a whiff of evil, an intuition that something is *wrong*. Mordecai Richler, for instance, doesn't write like Norman Mailer, but, as journalists, both are polemicists working out of a shared Jewish heritage. The pejorative words commonly used to describe journalists – scum, muckrakers, scandal-mongers – reflect the fact that we usually find ourselves journeying through the world's murkier waters.

A tradition is not a straitjacket, but imitating an inappropriate or antithetical model *is* a recipe for failure. It is necessary for writers not only to know who we are, but *where* we are. This, of course, is the point of keeping a journal.

FURTHER READING

Canadian Exploration Literature, an anthology edited by Germaine Warkentin, Oxford University Press. I have taken the excerpts from the journals of Radisson and Hearne from this excellent collection.

Hearne's *Journey* has also been published in several editions. Hearne's map-making skills have been criticized, but as a journalist he is a model to admire in all respects. A pleasure to read and reread.

Betty Friedan, *The Feminine Mystique*, Dell, 1963. A brilliant, revolutionary exposé of the North American housewife's suburban gulag.

The Jesuit Relations and Allied Documents, Carleton Library, McClelland & Stewart. Both Regnaut's account and the excerpt from LeJeune's *relation* are taken from this very abbreviated selection. The complete *Relations* fill libraries.

Lawrence Martin, *The Antagonist: Lucien Bouchard and the Politics of Delusion*, Penguin, 1997. Martin casts Quebec's separatist premier as the Sorcerer in a political drama where Bouchard plays the multiple roles of martyr, revolutionary, and Sun King. *Plus ça change. . . .*

CHAPTER 6

The Interior Journey

We tend to associate journalism with stories of exciting events in unusual places, but some of the best true stories are written by psychic mariners. Their purpose in recording the circumstances of their lives is to create a personal narrative, an interior map that will lead them towards intangible goals of self-knowledge, revelation, and reconciliation.

THE DIARY

The simplicity of the diary form deceives many writers. Buy a little notebook, a stubby pencil, and *voilà*! All your travels, adventures, and anecdotes are recorded for posterity, and you will have the raw material for a story or a book. Yet diaries rarely get finished, much less published, and when a diary is published, the writer's reputation may be ruined. Do you really want to do this?

In its most elementary form, a diary is a notation of daily events. The problem is: What events are worth noting? Why? A diary needs to have a purpose. A ship's captain keeps a log as a record of his voyage, a reason, perhaps, why diaries are associated with travel, but why does a passenger need to record the daily temperature, the height of the waves, or the exact time of arrival in port? What if nothing happens?

Diarists give up because they bore themselves with conventional detail, and fail to discriminate between trivial and significant events. The most obvious events are often the least important. Canadian painter Alex Colville's *Diary of a War Artist* (Nimbus, 1981) illustrates how a diary can evolve from impersonal jottings into an introspective meditation.

Colville, a twenty-four-year-old infantry officer assigned to duty as a war artist in 1944, began his diary on July 21, "so that I can tell Rhoda [his wife] in some detail of my experiences when I get back home." His motive was typical, and his second entry could have been written by any one of thousands of young officers: "Left Paddington 1355. Stood up most of way in 3rd class carriage. Arrived Cardiff 1800. By chance met Comd. Kelly an Admiralty Courier, who drove me to ship. Headache and starved. Comd. Kelly is Captain of *Prince David* – charming, impulsive man of action. Had a drink, stood and talked to 2100 – thought I would faint. Had a good meal but couldn't enjoy it. . . ."

Once Colville began to sketch and paint, however, his diary became a means of recording the work he completed each day, often under difficult circumstances, and since he was drawing hastily in ink or charcoal, he noted shades of colour he would later incorporate in paintings based on his sketches. His diary also began to reveal how he worked as an artist, and how he felt about it:

I stayed indoors on 9 January and completed *In a Dugout*, one of my most finished works. Most of the next day was spent arranging for my driver to go on leave, but in the afternoon I started *The Barrier* from a drawing, the weather being cold and snowy. The following morning I finished this picture, which I painted in watercolour and tempera on gray paper. That afternoon I painted *An Me 109 in Snow* from inside the jeep. The roof was covered with ice, which melted and leaked through after we lit the oil heater. It was snowing furiously outside and flakes infiltrated through the curtains, spotting the sky on my watercolour. In spite of these trials, the subject was so good (very bleak and colourless) that I felt fairly satisfied with the finished work.

In *Diary of a War Artist*, these excerpts accompany illustrations of the works Colville discusses, placing them within a narrative context that enriches their meaning. One of Colville's most difficult assignments was to sketch the victims of the Nazi concentration camp at Belsen, and he arrived on April 29, 1945, shortly after Belsen was liberated by Allied troops. "On the first day I made a drawing of some women, dead from starvation and typhus, lying outside one of the huts," he writes. "While I drew, the group of bodies was added to as more people died and were feebly dragged out of the hut by the inhabitants, who were themselves more dead than alive."

This passage is effective because of its understated, unemotional tone, and Colville explains why: "This being in Belsen was strange. The thing one felt was that one felt badly that one didn't feel worse. That is to say, you see one dead person and it is too bad, but seeing five hundred is not five hundred times worse. There is a certain point at which you begin to feel nothing."

Events in themselves, however bloody or gruesome, do not make a story. Colville's diary is a story of self-discovery: he began his war as a naive young soldier, and ended it a mature artist.

It may be the connection with warfare that gives the diary its aura of secrecy. A diary had to be small enough to stuff into a pocket, and too inconspicuous to attract the enemy's attention.

A war diary's information was crucial to winning battles, awarding medals, assigning blame in the event of defeat, and preserving the collective memory in case no one but the writer survived.

A war diary was the ideal medium for a clever but obscure young diplomat, Charles Ritchie, who spent most of the Second World War attached to the Canadian embassy in London, England. Ritchie revelled in gossip and intrigue, and *The Siren Years* (Macmillan Canada, 1974), the first and best of his published diaries, is to the diary what *Casablanca* is to film. It is, like *Casablanca*, a love story. Elizabeth, the mysterious heroine, appears rarely, but the fluttering and thumping of Ritchie's heart can be heard in his prose. Being bombed, on the other hand, brings out his sense of humour. Coming back from an overnight trip, Ritchie finds his apartment building reduced to a heap of rubble:

> I have lost everything I own. That is no tragedy but a bore – and doubtless a cash loss, as the Department of External Affairs will never approve replacing suits from Sackville Street at twenty pounds per suit. I am most annoyed at losing my new "woodsy" tweed suit, the picture of the Rose that Anne gave me, volume two of the book I am reading, my edition of Rimbaud and the little green book of my own chosen quotations. I do not much regret all the pigskin which used to jar on her so much.
>
> I am enjoying the publicity attendant on this disaster, particularly the idea which I have put abroad that if it had not been for a chance decision to go to Aldershot for the night I should have been killed. I should probably only have been cut about or bruised. The rest of the people living in the flats were in the cellar and escaped unhurt. The youth next door was full of the fact that Lord A and Lady A too had had to be pulled out of the debris – so had fourteen other people,

but what struck him was that even a lord had not been spared by the bomb. A further fascinating detail was that Lord A's naval uniform was still hanging on the hook on the open surviving wall for all the world to see. Now I know that the *Evening Standard* is right when it prints those items "Baronet's kinswoman in a bus smash," etc. I feel like a tramp having only one suit and shirt and in particular only *one pair of shoes.*

Most of us would scribble on and on, full of excitement and a sense of Great Events, but if Ritchie did, he wisely cut it all out of his manuscript. His economy of language and precision of detail, combined with his crankiness, convey a genuine impression of a man in shock. Ritchie understands perfectly the importance of leaving things to the reader's imagination. Being forced to solve puzzles – Who's Anne? What pigskin? – encourages us to turn the page to find the answer. What is left out of a diary is as significant as what is noted. The writer creates a persona – in this case the blasé man of affairs – that may have little to do with his actual circumstances.

Good diarists tend to be sociable people who feel like outsiders. They are egocentric, but insecure, introspective, yet concerned about how they appear to others. Ritchie, an anglophile from Nova Scotia, was acutely conscious of being an awkward colonial. This entry is typical: "One day I went out to the bus in my patent leather shoes and without a hat. Two girls in the street turned around and made some sort of crack. I felt ridiculous and humiliated. When I think of my youth it makes me angry even now. I feel I ought to have my own back at someone for all that vain, timid, harmless dreamer had to put up with. Now I have the weapons."

Writing well, they say, is the best revenge, and Ritchie's diary is enlivened by his acerbic comments about people who offend him (he includes himself). Snobs were one of his pet peeves. He describes meeting a new officer at the British Embassy, "a smooth-faced Etonian with an air of sophistication. What happens to them at Eton? However innocent, stupid, or honest they may be they always look as though they had passed the preceding night in bed with a high-class prostitute and had spent the earlier part of the morning smoothing away the ravages with the aid of creams, oils, and curling tongs."

This comment looks dashed-off, but it was probably the product of several hours of reflection. Sex was a major preoccupation with Ritchie, as it tends to be with successful diarists, and it may have been his inability to speak openly about it that attracted Ritchie to the "solitary vice" of keeping a diary. Clandestine *affaires* are perfectly suited to a secretive medium – some diarists write in code or shorthand – and they provide the writer with a ready-made plot to hold the fragments of daily events together.

A diary can be almost entirely a psychic voyage. This is true of the unpublished diaries of William Lyon Mackenzie King, prime minister of Canada for all but five years between 1921 and 1948, and the monumental diaries of bohemian writer Anaïs Nin, published in truncated form in a series of seven volumes beginning in 1966. A discreet selection of excerpts from King's diaries was published in a 1976 biography by historian C. P. Stacey, *A Very Double Life: The Private World of Mackenzie King* (Macmillan Canada, 1976).

In public life, King and Nin appeared to be such opposites they would have fled from each other at first sight, yet in writing their diaries they adopted an identical model: the psychiatrist's couch. Both were narcissists. The diary was a confidant to whom they could describe their dreams and fantasies, pour out their anxieties, express their self-pity, and justify their sexual behaviour. They are both narratives of compulsive seduction involving, in Nin's case, men and women, and, in both instances, they imply incest.

This recurrent Oedipal theme, expressed in often overwrought, hysterical prose, gives these diaries, for all their egoism and verbosity, an almost hypnotic fascination. Yet they are not confessions, because there is no expression of guilt, remorse, or personal responsibility. These two people admit, if only obliquely, the unspeakable source of their anguish and perverse behaviour, but since they can't do anything about it, they rewrite their lives as fairy tales, using the diary as a script.

Nin was a habitual liar, and she enjoyed a challenge. "Could I deceive a professional analyst?" she coyly asks her diary. She was seeing a psychiatrist, Dr. Allendy, in Paris, ostensibly to overcome her feelings of inadequacy, yet at the same time she was carrying on a torrid romance with novelist Henry Miller and his wife, June.

"I was still examining some of the stories I had told Allendy," she writes: "examining them for loopholes, defects. For he had demanded that I never see Henry or his friends or June again."

I said I had broken with them.

The secret of my lies must be that which makes for good acting. I never plunge into a lie carelessly, without first telling myself: "How would I feel if this were true?" (How would I feel if I had broken with Henry's world?) I start feeling and believing the situation. Also I have learned transpositions. I borrow from the distress caused me by June's behaviour and transfer this to the present. I have sometimes wished I could break with Henry's world. My hands are cold. I show symptoms of distress. Allendy can check that, but they have a different cause. However by this time I feel I have entered into my own story. (And I have, for the space of an hour.) And it is true I need Allendy. It touched me humanly that Allendy could no longer be objective.

The charm of this passage is its coldness, its smug sense of triumph. Nin, now bored by Miller and his wife, was using her erotic fantasies to seduce Allendy. "This diary is my kief, hashish, and opium pipe," she writes. "Instead of writing a novel, I lie back with this book and a pen, and dream . . . I must relive my life in the dream." If she saw herself as Scheherazade, Mackenzie King cast himself as Parsifal in Wagner's version of the Grail myth.

The striking thing about these diaries is their confident voice. The writer may throw up a smokescreen of bombast and purple prose, but behind it is an intelligent observer, worldly, self-reflective, determined to bring order into the chaos of everyday life. A diary is beyond morality. What happens, happens: a small notebook has no room for explanation or elucidation. It works best as a puppet show with familiar characters – the artist, the lover, the fool, the man of the world, the *femme fatale* – as long as the diarist is not afraid to be seen as a manipulative egomaniac.

THE JOURNAL

A diary is a mirror, a journal a window. A journal (which may be called a diary) is generally understood to be more expansive and reflective, a medium that encourages description, rumination, and speculation. A journal shows the writer participating in daily events. These events may be extraordinary – Samuel Pepys describes the devastation of London during the Great Fire – or domestic – E. B. White tenderly memorializes his dying pig.

White's essays, published for decades in *The New Yorker*, are models of personal narrative, although his laconic Yankee style, derived from Henry David Thoreau's classic *Walden*, may today seem quaint and contrived. White has the ability to analyze his own thoughts and emotions while giving the impression that he is having a casual chat with the reader, and he can turn a simple incident into a parable. This is from a 1941 essay, "On a Florida Key."

There are two moving picture theatres in the town. In one of them coloured people are allowed in the balcony. In the other, coloured people are not allowed at all. I saw a patriotic newsreel there the other day which ended with a picture of the American flag blowing in the breeze, and the words: one nation indivisible, with liberty and justice for all. Everyone clapped, but I decided I could not clap for liberty and justice (for all) while I was in a theatre from which Negroes had been barred. And I felt there were too many people in the world who think liberty and justice for all means liberty and justice for themselves and their friends. I sat there wondering what would happen to me if I were to jump up and say in a loud voice: "If you folks like liberty and justice so much, why do you keep Negroes from this theatre?" I am sure it would have surprised everybody very much and it is the kind of thing I dream about doing but never do. If I had done it I suppose the management would have taken me by the arm and marched me out of the theatre, on the grounds that it is disturbing the peace to speak up for liberty just as the feature is coming on. When a man is in the South he must do as the Southerners do; but although I am willing to call my wife "sugar" I am not willing to call a coloured person a nigger.

A good journalist has the ability to see that the emperor is wearing no clothes; in other words, there is a discrepancy between our illusions and the evidence before our eyes. (Does this explain why journalism is so obsessed with the British Royal Family, American presidents, Hollywood movie stars, and pop musicians?) The journalist is always the underdog, the humble, journeyman scribe who sees all, but goes unnoticed in the crowd. In Volume II of her *Selected Journals* (Oxford University Press, 1987), Lucy Maud Montgomery, the author of *Anne of Green Gables*, makes excellent use of this perspective in her account of meeting Canada's governor-general, Earl Grey:

Presently Earl Grey asked me to go for a walk, saying he wanted to hear all about my books etc. We went through the orchard and followed a little winding path past the trees until we came to a small white building. "Let's sit down here," said His Excellency, squatting down on the steps. Accordingly I "sat" too – since there did not exactly seem to be anything else I could do. I could not say to Earl Grey "This is the Macphail water closet" – although that is what it was!! I suppose Earl Grey didn't know there were such places in existence. It was a neat little building, painted white, and even had a lace curtain in the window – likely put on for the occasion. And that is where His Excellency and I sat for half an hour and had our heart to heart talk. He never let the conversation lag, for he could ask a "blue streak" of questions. He asked me to send him an autographed copy of *Kilmeny* and my poems and was altogether delightful to me. But I was suffering so acutely from a suppressed desire to laugh that I hardly knew what I was saying. The Earl thought I was nervous and asked me if I had been rather dismayed at the idea of meeting him and when I said, "Yes, I've been in a blue funk," he laughed and said "But you won't feel that way any more, will you?" I said "No," but I really think if we had sat there much longer I would have gone into hysterics – and never have been able to explain why. I was mortally afraid that some poor unfortunate was cooped up in the house behind us, not able to get out; and I beheld with fascinated eye straggling twos and threes of women stealing through the orchard in search of the W.C. and slinking hurriedly back when they beheld the Earl and me gallantly holding the fort!

Both examples show how a personal narrative can become a short story, with a cast of characters (including the author), drama, conflict, suspense, and a perfectly realized scenario. These stories are told in a powerful, commanding voice. It is not an introspective voice. This is how Montgomery describes her wedding banquet:

I had been feeling contented all the morning. I had gone through the ceremony and the congratulations unflustered and unregretful. And now, when it was all over and I found myself sitting there by my husband's side – *my husband* – I felt like a prisoner – a hopeless prisoner. Something in me – something wild and free and untamed – something that Ewan had not tamed – could never tame – something that did not acknowledge him as master – rose up in one frantic protest against the fetters which bound me. At that moment if I could have torn the wedding ring from my finger and so freed myself I would have done it! But it was too late – and the realization that it was too late fell over me like a black cloud of wretchedness. I sat at that gay bridal feast, in my white veil and orange blossoms, beside the man I had married – and I was as unhappy as I had ever been in my life.

Scholars still speculate about what could have prompted Montgomery, the vivacious young author of the *Anne* books and other popular romances, to enter into a loveless marriage with Ewan Macdonald, a small-town Presbyterian minister. Unhappiness, however, is rich material for a writer, and Montgomery anticipated that her journals would eventually be recognized as her most important work. Marriage, however, trapped her in stifling conformity, and unlike Stephen Leacock, she was too circumspect to exploit the satirical possibilities of her rural Ontario surroundings. Montgomery lacked empathy and a journalist's curiosity about other people's lives, and as her fame increased, she became more aloof and self-important. She donned the martyr's hair shirt, but refused to examine her soul. Some time after her wedding she wrote:

"It was a curious psychological experience which I shudder to recall. Never did I reach a blacker depth of despair and futile rebellion. It was so dreadful that it *could not* last. Either I must conquer it or die. I conquered it – thrust it down – smothered it – buried it. Whether dead or quiescent it has not troubled me since."

Far from being smothered, Montgomery's suppressed rage simmers with sulphurous fumes throughout Volume III of her journals. Her fury has many targets, but the chief victim is her hapless husband, who suffered from bouts of depression. On Tuesday, November 1, 1921, Montgomery writes:

I have been having a dreadful week of it. Ewan has had one of the worst attacks of his malady he has ever had – by far the worst this year. Poor Ewan, in these attacks, doesn't believe that he *has* any malady.

"I am perfectly well; but I am outcast from God. *That* is my trouble. You do not sympathize with me."

That is Ewan's attitude. I feel sick at heart. During the first summer of his melancholia I knew he was tortured by such thoughts but I did not think they had troubled him since. Oh, *can* I go on like this, with no one to advise or share the burden? Oh, religious melancholy is a hideous thing. Ewan seems to me like an absolute stranger in these attacks. He is no more like the man I married than – he is *not* the man I married. An altogether different personality is there – and a personality which is repulsive and abhorrent to me. And yet to this personality I must be a wife. It is horrible – it is indecent – it should not be. I feel degraded and unclean.

A sense of damnation was not out of place in a Presbyterian preacher, and given Montgomery's attitude, it's hardly surprising that Ewan suffered from periods of despair. It doesn't seem to have crossed Montgomery's mind that she might be the cause of Ewan's attacks, or that he was as lonely and miserable as she. Nor does it occur to her that she may be projecting on to Ewan her own chronic anxiety, depression, and fear of insanity.

Writing is a wonderful way to blow off steam. Don't be surprised if a lot of angry words and violent images appear on the page. Examine them. Where have they come from? Why? Whatever topic writers choose, we ultimately write about ourselves. Montgomery is a dramatic writer with an acute ear for conversation, but her journals are a cautionary tale – vengeful writers who reveal others' weaknesses may inadvertently expose their own.

THE MEDITATION

Keeping a journal may be a search for the meaning of life, and it's a traditional and popular way for writers to locate themselves in relation to Humanity, Nature, and God. In North America, the seminal example is Thoreau's *Walden*. Thoreau's description of his two years living at Walden Pond provides a structure for an extended essay on Goodness and Truth. "A lake is the landscape's most beautiful and expressive feature," he writes. "It is earth's eye; looking into which the beholder measures the depth of his own nature."

Thoreau's transcendentalism was derived from the French contemplatives, Pascal, Montaigne, and Rousseau, the English Romantic poets, especially Coleridge and Wordsworth, the aesthetics of John Ruskin, the rhetoric of Thomas Carlyle, New England Puritanism, and his own preoccupation with mortality: he died of tuberculosis at age forty-five, only eight years after *Walden* was published. To Thoreau, Nature's value was largely symbolic, but *Walden* has inspired a vast literature of romantic environmentalism: Annie Dillard's *Pilgrim at Tinker Creek* (HarperPerennial) is a recent example. This genre also includes books about spirituality, life after death, healing and wellness, angels, goddess worship, and women who run with wolves. Totems – wolves, coyotes, ravens, and owls – figure prominently, as do elders and shamans – Indians, Eskimos, hermits, or, in Thoreau's case, a French-Canadian lumberjack. God may be male or female, present or absent, but a meditation is distinguished by its mysticism and moralism, the search for an epiphany, a state of grace.

At its worst, a meditation can be a crock of pretentious twaddle. It relies for effect on an elevated, "poetic" language that is the antithesis of the journal's plain speech. Thoreau, who read and wrote poetry, composed *Walden* over a period of nine years, using his journals only as raw material. *Walden* has plenty of twaddle, but Thoreau brings it off with a passage like this: "Suddenly an influx of light filled my house, though the evening was at hand, and the clouds of winter still overhung it, and the eaves were dripping with sleety rain. I looked out the window, and lo! where yesterday was cold grey ice there lay the transparent pond already calm and full of hope as in a summer evening, reflecting a summer evening sky in its bosom, though none was visible overhead, as if it had intelligence with some remote horizon."

THE CONFESSION

The confessional narrative has its roots in the literature of the Christian church: *The Confessions of St. Augustine* (397–401) and Cardinal Newman's *Apologia pro vita sua* of 1864 are two famous examples. The confession presupposes a sense of sin, and since sin has largely disappeared as a concept in the post-Christian world, a confession has little meaning outside a court of law. Television has debased it into trivial chatter for the talk shows, and it is often a subtle excuse for self-congratulation.

In his *Confessions,* published in twelve volumes in the 1780s after his death, Jean-Jacques Rousseau admits to nothing more sleazy than petty crime, and he self-righteously portrays himself as a sensitive innocent beset by enemies. Much of Rousseau's narrative is gossip, his motive is revenge, and his tone is sycophantic. Rousseau's conscience is so clear, he boasts about abandoning his five infant children to an orphanage, an arrangement, he says, that "seemed good and sensible and right to me."

This tone of self-justification is characteristic of confessions, which also tend to be full of omissions and distortions of fact. For readers, a confession is fascinating for what it reveals about the writer's secret life and agitated emotional state, but for the writer, these revelations, while they may cause a *succès de scandale*, will not necessarily enhance, or create, a literary reputation.

"I was not magically saved from the pain of my childhood," Elly Danica says about the publication in 1988 of her book *Don't: A Woman's Word* (gynergy books), a personal revelation of incestuous sexual abuse so graphic one reviewer called it an "unyielding scream." In the sequel, *Beyond Don't* (gynergy, 1997), Danica writes:

At first I was appalled by people's reactions to *Don't*. People hurt and cried reading what I had written, which made me feel wretched. For several years, whenever I went to the city and was recognized, I would be either stared at and whispered about, or approached by people who had horrific childhood disclosures they wished to share with me. I am not hard-hearted. I would listen and offer what comfort I could. I would arrive home exhausted, angry and confused. The problem was that I was no longer seen as a person separate and apart from the book. I began to feel erased by this unbearably narrow view of who I was. The sum total of my identity seemed to be the experience I had described.

Public interest in a confession is prurient, and while the urge to reveal repulsive, addictive, or illegal behaviour may be overwhelming, beware of the consequences. If the writer does not corroborate the events from independent sources, or develop self-awareness, the story takes on the characteristics of a fantasy or nightmare, leaving the impression that the writer is a liar or a psychopath. On the other hand, as Danica points out, the story may turn into a monster that swallows the writer's identity.

THE MEMOIR

As the word implies, a memoir is an act of remembering the past. Since our memories are selective and untrustworthy, a memoir tends to be a highly imaginative recreation of events featuring the writer as hero. If the past is remembered as a Golden Age, the tone will be romantic and nostalgic, but a memoir may also be a bitter recollection of past hurts.

Essential to a successful memoir is a sense of loss: there is a dramatic break between the writer's present circumstances and the events remembered. Isak Dinesen's *Out of Africa* (Random

House, 1937), for instance, is a memorial to her failed farm, her dead lover, a dying colonial culture, and an African paradise threatened with annihilation. Circumstances don't always have to be this drastic. In his hockey memoir, *The Game* (Macmillan Canada, 1983), goalie Ken Dryden contemplates the impending end of his own career as his legendary team, the Montreal Canadiens, enters its twilight years.

A memoir, however, is not an obituary. An obituary is seldom written by the deceased, and convention demands, unfortunately, that we speak only good of the dead. A sentimental, self-serving recital of the "good old days," or uncritical praise of historical figures, turns the writer into a Boring Old Fart. This is particularly true of memoirs of the Second World War, which, like memoirs of the British Raj in India, are voluminous enough to form an entire sub-genre. In most of these recollections, the war is seen as a coming-of-age experience the writer looks back on with pride and satisfaction. Because there is nothing lost to mourn, the memories of dead comrades have a hollow ring, and the writer's egoism blows his own modest exploits out of proportion.

An exception is Farley Mowat's *And No Birds Sang* (McClelland & Stewart, 1979), a war memoir built on the universal theme of lost innocence. Mowat sees the moral conflict – kill or be killed – at the centre of the carnage, and has the capacity to identify with the victim, even when the victim is a Nazi. Mowat describes taking refuge from German rockets in a ruined stone hut:

> I reached it just as the bombs exploded a few score yards away. The blast flung me through the empty doorway with such violence that I sprawled full-length on top of a prone human figure who emitted a horrid gurgling belch. It was an unconscious protest, for he and two of his three companions – grey-clad paratroopers – were dead, their bodies mired in

the muck and goat manure on the floor. The fourth man –
dimly seen in that dim place – was sitting upright in a corner
of the little unroofed room and his eyes met mine as I strug-
gled to my hands and knees.

In that instant I was so convinced that this was death –
that he would shoot me where I knelt – that I did not even try
to reach for the carbine slung across my back. I remained
transfixed for what seemed an interminable time, then in an
unconscious reflex effort I flung myself sideways and rolled
to my feet. I was lurching through the doorway when his thin
voice reached me.

"Vasser . . . haff . . . you . . . vasser?"

I checked my rush and swung up against the outer wall,
knowing then that I was safe, that he posed no threat. And
I felt an inexplicable sense of recognition, almost as if I
had heard his voice before. Cautiously I peered back through
the doorway.

His left hand was clasping the shattered stump where his
right arm had been severed just below the elbow. Dark gore
was still gouting between his fingers and spreading in a black
pool about his outthrust legs. Most dreadful was a great gash
in his side from which protruded a glistening dark mass
which must have been his liver. Above this wreckage his eyes
were large and luminous in a young man's face, pallid to the
point of translucency.

"Vasser . . . please giff . . . vasser."

This passage shows the skill that has made Mowat an inter-
nationally celebrated writer. It is full of action – he is literally blown
in the door – and he uses his activity to draw out the suspense.
Mowat's imagery is tactile, visceral, and kinetic; he includes light,
sounds, and the implied smells of rotting bodies, muck, and goat

manure. He establishes a tense confrontation, then slows his narrative long enough to communicate his flash of relief and puzzled recognition. The phrase "grey-clad," followed later by a few words in German-accented English, establish the paratrooper's threatening identity, but the German's halting words elicit our sympathy. We share the conflicting emotions Mowat felt at the time.

With a careful choice of words, Mowat subtly deepens the significance of this encounter. The "fourth man" recalls the Fourth Horseman of the Apocalypse, and by repeating "dim" to emphasize the contrast between the light in the hut and the sun-scorched Italian hills outside, he creates the impression that the hut is a cave, almost a crypt. In the pallid figure in the corner, Mowat recognizes his Shadow, Death.

This memoir was published years after the war ended but, like most memoirs, it is based on notes Mowat made at the time. Very few people sit down at the age of seventy and say, "Okay, I'll write my memoirs." For decades they save letters, tax returns, and newspaper clippings; they transform their experiences into bedtime stories for their children, they scribble notes, they brood and they dream.

"This book was lived and researched over twenty-five years, thought about consciously on and off for at least the last five of those years, and finally written," Ken Dryden writes in the introduction to *The Game*.

It began as a boxful of scrap paper – hotel stationery, backs of envelopes, torn pages from newspapers and magazines – random inspirations that came to me from sleepless post-game nights, from twenty-two miles of silent highway from home to the Forum and back ("When am I going to remember to put a pen in that glove compartment?"), from games behind a peerless defence that often left me with nothing else to do. I was sure that, clipped together, filed, laid end-to-end, they would become a book. They did not. Like most midnight thoughts, what I found in the morning looked disturbingly thin and incomplete, often contradictory, not at all the story that had seemed to me so different and untold. Yet each scrap would later become a useful trigger for recollections otherwise lost.

Most sports memoirs never get past this two-by-four scaffolding stage, but it seems that during the pauses in the game when Dryden lounged in the goal crease, leaning on his stick, he pondered the sportscasters' perennial question, "How did it feel?" and decided the question needed a more considered response than "Unhh, great!"

He begins *The Game* improbably, but appropriately, in bed:

It has been a short, restless night, yet I feel wonderfully refreshed. The sun, the crisp white sheets, a quilt pulled up to my nose – I'm filled with an enormous sense of well-being and for several moments I don't know why. Then I remember. The game, last night's game in Buffalo. I must be tired – it's less than four hours since I went to bed – but that can wait. I want to be awake, I want to lie in my bed and feel the feeling I earned last night, to wrap my covers around it, to gather it up and hold it, to feel all of it *completely*.

The reflective, yet sensual tone of this opening passage establishes the intimate mood of Dryden's narrative, and his cosy surroundings allow him to shed his goalie persona and speak in his own voice. Like Dinesen and Mowat, Dryden avoids narcissism by using his memories as a window to view the world, rather than as a mirror to reflect his own virtues, and he has as many wise and funny things to say about his coaches and teammates as about himself.

Because it is a recollection in tranquillity, a memoir has a meditative, philosophical dimension readers don't expect from something written in haste, such as a diary or journal. *The Game* elevates the often vulgar, brutal rituals of hockey into a form of classical drama in which the fans participate as a raucous chorus.

Writers often make the mistake of thinking a memoir has to be about the rich or famous. In fact, Dryden's best anecdotes concern the humble players on the team, and the star of *Out of Africa* is Dinesen's African houseboy and cook, Kamante. Dinesen writes: "The Prince of Wales did me the great honour to come and dine at the farm, and to compliment me on a Cumberland Sauce. This is the only time that I have seen Kamante listening with deep interest when I repeated the praise of his cooking to him, for Natives have very great ideas of kings and like to talk about them."

So much for the Prince of Wales. *Out of Africa* contains not another word about him, but Dinesen writes chapters about Kamante. She entirely erases her nasty husband, Baron Blixen, and includes only those people she finds interesting. These characters don't have to be brilliant or charming: in *Halfbreed* (McClelland & Stewart, 1973), Maria Campbell writes about her rough-and-tumble backwoods childhood in a way that makes the natives of northern Saskatchewan as fascinating as Dinesen's Natives.

Since a memoir demands powers of almost total recall, the trick is knowing what to throw out. What memories do you want to share with strangers, and why? Do you want to create an elegiac mood, or are you well rid of the past? What role do you play in the memoir? Too many memoirs are written by people to whom nothing much happens, or they place too much emphasis on a conventional childhood, or they fail to get beneath superficial appearances. A memoir mourns or celebrates a lost relationship, and by reconstructing the past it combines elements of history, fiction, and biography. This delicate balance can be difficult to achieve, especially when your memoir is about somebody else.

BIOGRAPHY

A biography is usually written after the subject's death, either as a memorial, or to satisfy popular curiosity about the private life of a public figure. Biographers often begin their research while the subject is still living – James Boswell stuck like a burr to Samuel Johnson for twenty years – but it's risky to publish the biography while the subject is around to censor or condemn. We never see ourselves as others do, and, like the blind man feeling the elephant, every biographer has a different interpretation. Johnson himself said:

"The business of the biographer is often to pass slightly over those performances and incidents which produce vulgar greatness, to lead the thoughts into domestick privacies, and display the minute details of daily life."

Boswell, whose *Life of Samuel Johnson*, first published in 1791, remains a model of its kind, was fearful that his friendship with Johnson might interfere with his judgement. "He will be seen as he really was," Boswell firmly announces in his preface, "for I profess to write, not his panegyrick, which must be all praise, but his Life; which, great and good as he was, must not be supposed to be entirely perfect." Boswell then quotes Johnson's own advice, as valid today as it was then:

"If the biographer writes from personal knowledge, and makes haste to gratify the publick curiosity, there is danger lest his interest, his fear, his gratitude or his tenderness, overpower his fidelity, and tempt him to conceal, if not to invent. If we owe regard to the memory of the dead, there is yet more respect to be paid to knowledge, to virtue, and to truth."

Boswell, one of the most gifted and tenacious journalists who ever lived, took Johnson at his word. Boswell describes his first visit to Johnson's rooms: "He received me very courteously: but, it must be confessed that his apartment and furniture, and morning dress, were sufficiently uncouth. His brown suit of cloaths looked very rusty: he had on a little old shrivelled unpowdered wig, which was too small for his head; his shirt-neck and knees of his breeches were loose; his black worsted stockings ill drawn up; and he had a pair of unbuckled shoes by the way of slippers. But all these slovenly particularities were forgotten the moment that he began to talk."

Johnson was garrulous and gregarious, and ambitious young Boswell saw the literary potential of recording the famous scholar's epigrams, opinions, and gossip. When conversation flagged, Boswell would provoke an argument, or goad Johnson into a fit of vituperative rage. As their friendship grew, he pestered Johnson for personal information, chided him about his vulgar manners, cajoled him out of depressions, and tolerated his periods of pigheaded pomposity. Boswell, Pygmalion-like, *created* his subject. Johnson, with full knowledge and acquiescence, became his biographer's work-in-progress.

Boswell's intimacy with Johnson allowed him to write his *Life* with a tone of both authority and affection. It's vitally important to *like* your subject. You are asking your readers to spend time with this person, and who wants to waste time on a creep? A biographer's worst nightmare is discovering, when your research is well underway, that you really detest this person. What to do?

Admit it. Don't pretend. You may be able to shift focus to a more sympathetic character in the same story, or turn your biography into a memoir or social history. You could write a denunciation, or emphasize your subject's faults until they reach monstrous proportions. If you feel totally alienated and unhappy, you and your subject may be incompatible. The safest solution is to drop the project.

Biographers bring more emotional freight to their stories than they realize. Some appear to be motivated by envy, malice, or personal grievance, and they savage their subjects or praise them with faint damns. Be careful that *you* don't turn out to be the creep. Anger, guilt, and resentment are common aspects of bereavement, and perhaps for this reason, most family biographies are disguised as fiction or drama. Strong emotions, on the other hand, can spice up a biography. Look at this anecdote from Linda Frum's biography of her mother, radio and television broadcaster Barbara Frum. (*Barbara Frum: A Daughter's Memoir*, Random House, 1996):

One vivid memory [my brother] David and I share: As young school children we were on strict orders from our mother not to cross the major intersection that separated our grade school from our home until the housekeeper-of-the-moment came to guide us. Twice a day, at lunch and after school, we would walk to this point and stand shoulder to shoulder, silently staring at our warm house, so tantalizingly close. We'd wait and wait, pull our hands into our snowsuits and curl our toes inside our boots. Often the street would be barren of traffic and yet, obediently, we would stand, pathetically following mother's orders. It was not unusual for the housekeeper to become so engrossed in her soap opera that she would forget us altogether. As our noses and toes froze we could not help grumbling: "Why does Mummy have to work?"

The chilling thing about this orphans-in-the-storm picture is not neglect but *control*, and, as the rest of the book reveals, control was central to Barbara's personality. Linda grew into a rebellious daughter, and her relationship with Barbara was often tempestuous, yet when she began her biography after her mother's death from leukaemia in 1992, she felt only respect, love, and grief. When she showed her manuscript to David to check her own memories against his, he observed: "You seem very upset that you were left alone."

Linda was astonished. "I was *oblivious* to that," she says. "I had felt angry at the time, but I didn't feel angry now. David's comments triggered a greater level of examination of my feelings." Linda refused to deny her anger – it crackles like electricity through the book – but she was able to gain distance, and view her mother's life more from Barbara's own perspective. Her portrait is ambiguous, sometimes scary, but then so was Barbara Frum.

We biographers often suffer from not knowing enough about our prospective subjects. They or their executors may have destroyed all their personal papers, and their friends, family, and colleagues, if they are still alive, may be hostile. Never assume families will be cooperative. Relatives may resent the intrusion of a stranger, or have their own reasons for protecting the family's reputation. It may take time for them to get used to the idea, or to be convinced that you are the best person for the job. A writer I know was hired to write the biography of a prominent businessman; the family suddenly changed its mind, and she was paid a handsome fee *not* to write the book.

Don't give up simply because the most obvious archival sources come up empty. Fragments of documents are full of clues about where missing material might be. The documents may have been donated by someone very close to your subject, and a

single letter can hint at an important relationship. Ask the librarian or archivist about other sources. Once they understand your
interest, they may have suggestions. Things turn up in odd places
– kitchen cupboards, furnace rooms, cottages – and although
others may have looked at this material before you, they may not
have understood its significance.

It may happen that you find a mountain of raw material. On two
occasions, I have rooted through boxes of unsorted papers equivalent to the contents of a dumpster. The first time, I was harassed
by my subject's ferocious sister, intent on denying me access to
material she considered scandalous. I persevered – it was good
stuff! – but as I read, I came to dislike my subject almost as much
as I did her sister. The work was thankless, so I quit. Years later,
somebody else wrote the book. The second time, I hung in. I was
tracking down family and corporate collections scattered from
Ontario to Michigan, New Jersey, and Bermuda. My research took
me a year longer than I'd anticipated, but I found the paper trail so
fascinating I couldn't stop.

Writing about another person's life demands a long-term
commitment, and even uncomplicated biographies take years to
research and write. Every lead must be followed, facts checked
scrupulously, and information weighed for authenticity and bias.
Persuading people to talk about sensitive or embarrassing personal
details requires patience and charm, and you will have to confront
unsolvable puzzles and gaps in the narrative when the trail of
information simply disappears.

In such situations, admit the problem. If you cannot reconcile
two conflicting versions of events, give them both. If you don't
know, say so. There's nothing wrong with asking a question and
leaving it at that. The reader will have something to think about.
You may have grounds for speculation, but too much speculation
undermines your authority and interrupts your story. The reader

is interested in the person you are writing about, not in what you think. A biographer should be unobtrusive, and respect for the subject must be balanced by a healthy dose of scepticism. Before you can begin to put your story together, it may be necessary to demolish myths and fabrications, or even to throw out everything you had assumed about this person. If you find startling information, you may have to reassess your take on your subject. The worst mistake a biographer can make is to reject everything that doesn't fit with a preconceived theory or image.

Shaping a life into a story poses more problems. What is significant? What should you leave out, and why? Too often, biographers ignore Johnson's advice and write about the public figure, not the private person. They also err on the side of caution, suppressing information they feel may hurt others or damage their subject's reputation. In her biography of Barbara Frum, Linda glossed over her mother's estrangement from her adopted son, Matthew. It was a painful subject, and Linda was fearful Matthew would be hurt by having his troubled childhood exposed. As it turned out, Matthew didn't mind at all, and he resented having his role in the family drama diminished.

"I assumed I knew what he would feel," Linda admits. "It was a mistake." If you are worried about how people are going to take what you write about them, the best course is to check the quotes or passages with them in advance. They might correct errors, or give their version of the story. If they attempt to censor, you can ignore them, and if they threaten to sue, you're warned. Few people insist on being left out of a good story.

The hardest task is answering the question: Who *was* this person? Choose incidents and anecdotes that reveal character and emotion. Show your subject in a dramatic context. Quarrels, love affairs, temptations, and struggles with adversity are the warp and woof of good biography. Many biographers find a literary

archetype to use as a model: hero, rogue, renegade. Phyllis
Grosskurth called her recent biography of Lord Byron *The Flawed
Angel* (Macfarlane Walter & Ross, 1997).

Don't despair if your subject is secretive, evasive, a hard nut to
crack. Your struggle may be your story. "I was haunted by the
mystery of Gwendolyn," Rosemary Sullivan writes in *Shadow
Maker: The Life of Gwendolyn MacEwen* (HarperCollins, 1995).
MacEwen, a brilliant, prolific poet, whose youthful promise faded
into poverty and alcoholism, died at age forty-six in 1987. Sullivan,
a poet and scholar, had admired MacEwen but known her only
slightly, and MacEwen's personal papers seemed to Sullivan "like a
coded cryptogram culled of private details." Rather than attempt-
ing to explain this enigma, Sullivan decided to explore it:

> How to write about Gwendolyn, who kept herself so hidden,
> and how to discover why that hiding was necessary? I decided
> to follow the clues as they came, recording the voices that
> surrounded her, all those versions of her life she left behind.
> It would mean that I would not be able to pretend, as biog-
> raphers sometimes so, that one can turn a childhood into a
> seamless narrative when one is following forty years after
> the fact and constructing a childhood from the multiple
> versions of the survivors who are left behind. I would have
> to track down lost lovers, from whom there would be no
> letters and whom friends remembered only as a shadow or
> a name. Even then who was to say that the man I would
> meet and the man Gwendolyn had loved bore even the
> slightest resemblance to each other? What debris had gath-
> ered in the pockets of memory? To be faithful to the mystery
> that was Gwendolyn, I would have to lay bare the bones of
> my search for her, with little of the biographer's illusions or
> omniscience or objectivity.

Sullivan constructs *Shadow Maker* like a Greek tragedy, a counterpoint (in the musical sense) of keening and dispassionate voices with Sullivan acting as playwright and chorus, and it's an appropriate model for a story about a poet who mythologized her life. MacEwen's life – her psychotic mother, her addictions, and her self-destructive selection of lovers – was as theatrical as her persona, but Sullivan goes further, elevating MacEwen to "emblematic" stature as a Sophoclean heroine, "a woman of courage who, with those luminous eyes, faced down her life at the end of the twentieth century."

Well, okay. But other biographers would describe MacEwen as a peripheral figure, a fragile psyche destroyed by her own demons, and on the two or three occasions I met MacEwen, I was surprised to find her very Celtic, freckle-faced and funny. Sullivan is declaring her bias, telling us that the Gwendolyn MacEwen of *Shadow Maker* is her own witch/goddess, a literary construct drawn from MacEwen's poems and Sullivan's meticulous research.

AUTOBIOGRAPHY, LIFE WRITING, AND JOURNALING

Following the publication in the late 1960s of Bertrand Russell's two-volume *Autobiography* (Little, Brown), the autobiography, as it had been practised for centuries, fell out of fashion. Russell, an English aristocrat, mathematician, philosopher, lecher, gossip, pacificist, and political agitator, was also a brilliant writer, and his life story, which spanned ninety-seven years, set an impossible standard. Fearful imitators hired ghost-writers, others resorted to harrumphing or took refuge in the more modest memoir. Part of the blame for the form's decline must also rest with the writer who established the prototype, sixteenth-century artist and Renaissance man Benvenuto Cellini. In his classic *Autobiography*,

Cellini wrote: "In a work like this there will always be found occasion for natural bragging." Cellini had plenty to brag about, but once the autobiography was taken over by lesser politicians, generals, and business executives, it became the voice of the Dead White Male.

Today, the term "life writing" is often used as a user-friendly substitute for memoir, diary, or autobiography. It is less intimidating, and encourages free expression. As practised, however, life writing has developed conventions of its own. It tends to be practised in groups – writing workshops, classrooms, therapy sessions – where participants read or tell their stories aloud to each other and bounce ideas back and forth. As a result, the stories tend to be short, anecdotal, and confessional.

This method, while it encourages participants to express their emotions and write in their own voices, has its drawbacks. Worst is the attitude: "I'm okay, you're okay." If every life, and therefore every story, is given equal value, the workshop may make you feel better, but you won't learn anything about writing.

Life writing is an avenue of expression for people who feel marginalized, oppressed, angry, or ignored. (Life writing is, for instance, a staple of women's studies courses.) Telling your story is an act of liberation. Publishing is not the goal, although many of these stories do eventually appear in magazines and books. Life writing is also attractive to writers from oral cultures who are uncomfortable with formal English prose, or to people who want to write English in their own way. Here is the opening passage from "Some tings lie so deep," a story by Denise Barnard published in *Prairie Fire* magazine:

> The way we stand, my mother and I, side by side at the kitchen counter, reminds me of the lab experiments we carried out in high school science class. However we are conducting an

experiment of a different kind. Ours spans generations – the ones long dead and those yet to be born.

Lesson #1: "We call it pepper pot. Not because it full up o'pepper, mekking it too hot for our mout. Maybe we just do it to be extra, what you call showin' off. The other islands call it *callaloo*. But I always prefer pepper pot. Me no know why." Mama says all this, as if trying to explain why she likes the colour red better than blue.

"I can't Mama. I can't eat anymore. Please don't make me."

"Eh, eh. But what is dis? Ain't got no room for me food, dis food me slave over, but you never tired o'eatin' dem hot dogs, hamburgers, French fries, dem people's food. Wha' happen? You forget where you born? You goin' eat it even if it kill you."

But what's wrong with *their* food? Why can't we be like them? Why do we have to do everything differently? You can buy a hot dog anywhere, but where can you find plantain and codfish?

Mama pats her stomach and smiles: "We love our food back home. Not because we greedy guts, 'cause is only time we all be together. We laugh, talk, sing, shout, most of all eat."

The history of food weighs heavily upon my mother – in the 50 pounds she's been struggling to lose for as long as I can remember. "Me try and try, but me no can." Thanks to her greedy cancer, she's having no trouble these days.

Barnard uses language to counterpoint cultures and to express the existential conflict between mothers and daughters. Cooking the pepper pot becomes a ritual of remembering and reconciliation, and their shared, unspoken awareness of death gives the act of cooking a grieving, ironic edge.

My big trouble with this story is that the girl is named Jewel, or Julie. Where's Denise? In her introduction to this issue of *Prairie Fire* (Vol. 16, No. 3), entirely devoted to life writing, editor Helen Buss describes the contents as "autobiography and biography," but then hedges with words like "postmodern" and "geograficitone." Whazizz? My trust in the truth of Barnard's plainspoken story, and the rest of the collection, is shattered.

There is one exception, Valorie Bunce's "Body Hymn," an autobiography of her body.

> The Penis
> 1.
> I don't have one.
> 2.
> Don't remember envying them.
> 3.
> Always thought they were kinda funny looking. Like a nose, a Jimmy Durante nose. Like a long loose nose, wrinkled and pouchy.
> 4.
> It was part of my Dad, my Dad had one, has one still, I guess. Must, or I'm sure we'd have heard about it, families being what they are. Still has one, of course, or he'd be telling us how much trouble he has peeing.
> Cause men pee from it, take a leak they say, water my horse they say, have a piss they say. (The horses one always made me curious.)
> 5.
> When I was little Dad was big and scary. He was a big man, lots of muscle, big with big fat fingers and a big voice and a big dink too. I saw him once, accidentally, in the bathroom

and it was all very mysterious to me. What dads have. Mysterious and something to do with grunts and man-ness. And I think Dad felt the weight of being big and scary, cause altho he had a real temper and could yell with the best of them and could spank with his big hand too, there was really no reason to be afraid. At least that's the way I saw it, and that's how I reasoned it all out in my head when I was six or seven and decided that I wouldn't be afraid when he yelled. So I wasn't. And a funny thing happened. He stopped yelling and looked at me and then walked away. And it was a funny thing because it seemed to me he was glad I wasn't scared of him.

Bunce combines elements of poetry, drama, music, stream-of-consciousness, and stand-up comedy to achieve a coherent, sensual, and unusual perspective on her life. She uses her body parts to trigger free association about her experiences, and while the effect runs the risk of claustrophobia (do I really want to be inside someone else's body?) it's an imaginative switch from the solemn self-analysis of so much autobiographical writing.

There's a common belief that writing, in itself, is therapeutic. It can be, I guess. It can also create anxiety, guilt, and a feeling of failure. Life writing, however, appears to serve a therapeutic purpose for people who belong to the marginalized subculture of the sick (the mentally ill tend to write fiction and poetry). There is a massive literature about surviving cancer, near-death experiences, and healing journeys. Much of it is fiction, fantasy, quackery, or cultism. Some stories are witty or upbeat, but stories written as personal catharsis run the risk of sentimentality and emotional exploitation – Look at me, I'm suffering! People who really *are* suffering find it hard, even impossible, to get coherent words down on paper.

Writing won't cure anybody, but it can be a good way to get things off your chest, enlighten the public, and make sense of irrational, incoherent experience. Penelope Williams calls her personal account of breast cancer, *That Other Place* (Dundurn, 1993), "a travelogue, reports filed from a new and hostile land." She shapes her narrative around the underworld imagery of Virgil's *Aeneid*, but since her story has a happy ending, she includes hilarious anecdotes in the style of Chaucer's *Canterbury Tales*.

Williams's journal begins as an effort to cope with the nausea she suffered after chemotherapy: "At about my fourth treatment, in a vain attempt to get the feeling under control, I tried to go through it and by so doing, reach some kind of acceptance of it. I wrote down a description of exactly how I felt: 'The nausea is a visible, tangible entity now, a malevolent creature that has taken up residence in my throat. It is a dead/live thing, a lump of sweet, putrefying, wet decay, a small animal with matted stinking fur, an evil malignant presence. Although it's dead, I taste its foul breath when I breathe.'"

Williams's nausea doesn't go away, but by using kinesthetic imagery – the matted fur is a Surrealist touch – she makes the reader feel like throwing up too. By observing, taking notes, asking questions, researching medical literature, and listening to her fellow patients, Williams is able to gain perspective until she sees herself as the helpless heroine of a play or movie, unsure whether it's a comedy or tragedy. She describes her first radiation treatment this way:

"I lay down on the stretcher as directed, full of apprehension. The looming monster of the machine clicked over me as the nurses adjusted the sites. Four people then drew all over me with purple felt pens. Death by paint-by-number.

"After defining the target area, measuring and remeasuring,

muttering numbers, recalculating them and flicking the lights on and off, they all hustled out of the room leaving me exposed to the glare of the beast. I felt like a sacrifice lying on the altar of cancer; before the blow fell, the high priests had all raced from the church."

Williams draws on many literary traditions here, from the death of Iphigenia to *Beowulf* and *The Scarlet Letter*, but her contemporary imagery – "paint-by-number" – adds a raw edge of satire. Are we watching *Joan of Arc* or *The Perils of Pauline*? Williams describes the thoughts that were racing through her mind:

"Psychologically, radiation transforms you from a person – an individual with rights and feelings and emotions – into a slab of poisoned meat. After the technicians drew their indelible target on me, I felt like a carcass with the purple-inked inspection stamp blurred on my flesh. This feeling intensified when they started to cover my exposed breast with Saran Wrap. To keep the target forms clean, they said. I just felt microwaved."

Fear gives Williams a sharp ear for the callous chatter of doctors and nurses, and an eye for the ugliness and indignities of cancer treatment, but it is the pulse of her cold, controlled rage that drives her narrative forward. Williams was a writer and editor before she became a cancer patient – writing for her was an instinctive response – and like Aleksandr Solzhenitsyn in his 1968 novel *Cancer Ward*, she possessed the skills to transform her personal trauma into a literary artefact. She also wrote *That Other Place* after her treatments had succeeded. At first, she writes, "black, paralyzing depression shut down the runways of my brain like fog at an airport."

Life writing, or "journaling," as it's sometimes called, has become part of an array of therapies available to people suffering from cancer, AIDS, and other illnesses. Workshops are usually led by a professional therapist, who may also be a writer, and they vary according to the therapist's technique, personality, and philosophy.

In this context emphasis is, or should be, on *therapy*. For people in a state of panic, the discipline of putting words on paper may help them organize their lives and express taboo emotions.

"Journaling saved my life," says Marcia Loynd, who became a writing therapist after being treated for cancer in 1987. "I couldn't stop writing." Unlike other therapists, who encourage the sick to write memoirs or autobiographies, Loynd believes that a journal should deal only with the present. "Get it outside of yourself, then burn it if you like," she advises. "If you're not writing about what's going on, you get rooted in the past." In her workshops at Toronto's Wellspring centre for people with cancer, Loynd teaches techniques useful to all writers – sensory and self-awareness, free association, word play, emotional honesty, plain speech – but no literary skill is required and the journals are confidential unless participants choose to read passages aloud.

Not being judged was important to Wellspring journalist Mary Jane McKeen: "When I was diagnosed with cancer, a girlfriend gave me a blank book and said, 'Why not write?' 'Oh yeah, sure,' I said. 'I'm not writing in any book.' I was too angry, too upset. I was terrified. Then when I learned it was not *creative* writing, I gave it a try. I found it a wonderful way to vent my emotions. I could swear, draw awful pictures. I could let 'er rip, and I wouldn't be edited, no one would criticize me."

McKeen found that as she worked through her anger, her journal changed. "It became my security blanket when I went for radiation treatments. Writing in it was a way of talking to myself, telling myself to calm down, stay focused, not to panic. I couldn't concentrate to read, and the journal was a very concrete, hands-on thing to do. I didn't have to burden another human being with my feelings, yet I felt that I wasn't alone."

Our best book may be the one that keeps us alive.

FICTION, IN FACT

At what point does a writer's inventiveness overwhelm, or distort, the truth? Defining truth is a perennial bone of contention for writers and readers. A writer influences a story simply by choosing it, and a writer's intervention determines how the story will evolve. We all ask different questions, and relate to people in different ways; a story will be influenced as much by a writer's presence and personality as by the subject matter. The truth "as I see it" is about the best we can do.

Obviously it's not a good idea to write a story about an eight-year-old heroin addict if you have never clapped eyes on this kid. It's a terrific way of dramatizing a story about drug addiction, but it could have unforeseen repercussions. True stories shape events. This is why it's so important to name the people in your story: readers justly suspect that an unidentified source may not exist.

Readers will accept fictional stories involving real people – the historical romance is as old as history – but they *hate* a true story sprinkled with fictional characters or incidents. At the same time, they insist that your story be as entertaining as a novel, movie, or play.

One trick is to get *inside* your characters. Drop the role of journalist. Disappear. Internalize your research to the point where you no longer come between the story and the reader. I experimented with this technique in a biography of Isabella, the first wife of Canada's first prime minister, Sir John A. Macdonald:

Isabella Clark rearranged the lace collar on her new blue silk dress for the hundredth time that morning. She felt embarrassed, all decked out in her Sunday best in the middle of the week, but her sister Margaret had persuaded her, saying that the blue exactly matched her eyes, and besides, how often did they have company? Almost never, to tell the truth. The sisters' stone farmhouse, Ballafreer, was three miles from the village of Douglas on the Isle of Man in the middle of the Irish Sea, and the three sisters, Margaret, Isabella, and Jane, lived there alone. Their only regular callers were the local tradesmen, but in the spring of 1842 a letter from Canada disrupted the quiet routine of their lives: their cousin, John Alexander Macdonald, would be arriving at the end of June.

I wasn't in that stone farmhouse on a June day in 1842, and I was being very presumptuous to imagine what Isabella was thinking and feeling, but from having read Isabella's fragmentary letters, I felt confident about her voice and the way she thought. I also knew from my research that Macdonald's marriage to Isabella had been arranged by his family, with the cooperation of her sister Margaret, and that, unknown to him, Isabella, who suffered from mysterious pains, was in the early stages of opium addiction.

Isabella pressed her forehead against the cool glass of the window. An hour until ship time. The ticking of the grandfather clock reverberated in the silent parlour. She held her icy hands over her heart and took a deep breath. Maybe John wouldn't come. Maybe he would miss the boat. No, no, the disappointment of not seeing him would be worse. After all, he wasn't a suitor. She had given up on that. She was over thirty, a penniless orphan without a dowry. Isabella didn't blame eligible young men for turning their attention else-where, but she felt guilty about being so totally dependent on Margaret's charity.

I wrote these passages imitating the style of an early Victorian novel, conjuring up genteel life as it was lived in 1842, but every word was chosen to convey essential information about Isabella's appearance, health, family circumstances, social class, personality, and motives for marrying Macdonald. I created a nervous mood of anticipation, and made Isabella's meeting with Macdonald as dra-matic as my sparse resources permitted.

This is imagining, but it's not fiction. Between these two pas-sages, I inserted a paragraph in my own voice: "The Macdonalds had left Scotland for Kingston, Ontario, in 1820 when John was five and Isabella eleven. Had they met? It was unlikely. Their mothers were half-sisters, but the families were not close. Isabella's mother had married a captain in the British army, but Helen Macdonald had married badly, and beneath her. Hugh Macdonald was in trade, a rough Highlander with a weakness for whiskey and no head for business. Hugh's successive bankruptcies had reduced the family to penury, and John, the Macdonald's only son, was appren-ticed as a clerk at the age of fifteen to support the family. He was a lawyer now, but from what Isabella had heard, lazy and something of a roustabout."

This is straightforward exposition, but by using phrases Isabella might have used, "in trade" and "beneath her," I created the illusion that these thoughts were passing through her mind, and reinforced this perspective with the phrase, "from what Isabella had heard."

When the biography was published, one critic, a sociologist, chastised me for taking liberties. None of my readers complained. Whew. Imagining has to be done with care and caution. It can get out of control. In his jacket notes to *Fear and Loathing in Las Vegas and Other American Stories*, Hunter S. Thompson describes his title story as failed Gonzo journalism – he went over the brink into fiction. Still, it's a terrific story, and, as Thompson says, only an idiot would think it was true.

"On occasion," says Farley Mowat, "I have taken something that I have heard about and I have reworked it in my own mind until I was almost sure it had happened to me." Mowat's imaginative leaps have made him a controversial figure.

For Mowat, the story is all. "I never let the facts get in the way of the truth," he likes to say, and describes himself as "a simple saga man, a teller of tales." Using his powers of visualization, Mowat is able to visit places he has never been, witness things he has not seen with his own eyes, and imagine adventures which did not happen to him. He described his method to John Goddard in the May 1996 issue of *Saturday Night*: "*People of the Deer* is full of factual errors, lots of them, no argument about that. And full of elaborations. I didn't have all the information so I elaborated on it, and produced what I perceived to be the proper version of the way it had happened."

Critics call Mowat's "elaborations" fabrications, or lies, and it is impossible to tell which incidents in *People of the Deer* are real, exaggerated, distorted, or imagined. Mowat ruthlessly eliminates anything that doesn't contribute directly to the story he wants to tell. He describes his trip to the Arctic this way:

On a morning in May of 1947 I boarded the train and gave myself up to the demands of the fever that was in me. My preparations for the journey were simple in the extreme. A visit to a War Assets store had provided me with an assortment of old army clothing and a cheap sleeping bag. I already owned a camera of the snapshot variety and this, together with my binoculars and a dozen rolls of film, completed my scientific equipment. For weapons I took only the American carbine I had carried all through the war.

My actual plans were almost as shadowy as my equipment, for though I knew to within a few thousand square miles where I wanted to go, I still had only the vaguest ideas how to get there. I intended to travel alone. . . .

A romantic picture, but not true. In fact, Mowat had been hired as the junior partner in a well-financed scientific expedition organized by an American biologist, Francis Harper. The two men had a destination, a trapper's cabin at Nueltin Lake, and they flew there together, with six months of supplies, on a chartered plane.

Mowat was picturing himself in Vilhjálmur Stefánsson's heroic role, but his illusions about the self-reliant Eskimo were quickly shattered. He found squalor, hunger, and a population decimated to the point of extinction by epidemic diseases. Mowat did not live with the Eskimo, as his book implies – he seems to have gleaned much of his information from a trapper he calls Franz – and did not witness starvation, but he perceived the devastating impact of white civilization on the traditional Arctic way of life. By 1952, when *People of the Deer* was published, some Eskimo settlements *were* experiencing starvation, and tuberculosis had become catastrophic.

Mowat may have been wrong, even deliberately wrong, in his facts, but he argues, and I tend to agree, that *People of the Deer* is true in spirit. Mowat is really writing about himself, expressing his guilt, shock, and anger at the behaviour of *his own* people. He got his message across: *People of the Deer* and its sequels, *The Desperate People* and *Never Cry Wolf*, have sold millions of copies.

Like parables, Mowat's books should not be taken at face value. Mowat's critics complain that his inaccuracies and inventions or allegories made a bad situation worse – starvation has been succeeded by solvent-sniffing and suicide in some Inuit communities – but it is not a writer's role to be an economist, social worker, or politician.

I think Mowat could have written a factually accurate book as good as, or better than, *People of the Deer*. Who knows? For writers, the ultimate test is whether or not our stories are believed. Mowat's stories are believed.

FURTHER READING

Boswell's *London Journal*, McGraw-Hill. An intimate diary and an indispensable companion to his *Life* of Johnson. Also a social history of venereal disease in the eighteenth century.

Sharon Butala, *The Perfection of the Morning*, HarperPerennial, 1994. Like Thoreau, Butala uses nature as a landscape and a metaphor for her spiritual journey.

Elspeth Cameron, *No Previous Experience*, Viking, 1996. A hair-raising example of writing for revenge, and a lesbian coming-out confessional in the tradition of English writer Radclyffe Hall's *The Well of Loneliness*. If you have friends who keep diaries, treat them *very well*.

Donald Creighton, *Sir John A. Macdonald: The Young Politician*, Macmillan Canada, 1952; and *The Old Chieftain*, Macmillan Canada, 1955. Today, Creighton's pontifical style seems old-fashioned, but his numerous popular, opinionated books forged a new bond between history, journalism, and polemic. Creighton remains a pillar of Canadian scholarship and literature.

William Lyon Mackenzie King, "Diaries." King's diaries, which cover fifty-three years of his personal and public life, can be read in typed transcript at the National Archives of Canada, or on microfiche at major research libraries. Scholars who venture into the haunted labyrinth of King's psyche emerge looking like the figure in Edvard Munch's painting, *The Scream*. Well worth the trip. It's about time the diaries were annotated and published in their entirety.

Gelsey Kirkland (with Greg Lawrence), *Dancing on my Grave*, Jove. A classic example of a celebrity confessional that is also an exposé of the seamier side of the ballet world.

T. E. Lawrence, *Seven Pillars of Wisdom*, Jonathan Cape, 1926. A hypnotic memoir about Lawrence of Arabia's adventures in the Middle East.

Stephen Leacock, *Arcadian Adventures With the Idle Rich* and *Sunshine Sketches of a Little Town*, McClelland & Stewart. These satires are generally considered fiction, but I found them shelved under non-fiction in my local library. Leacock's characters and events were so recognizable that his home town of Orillia, Ontario, remains offended to this day.

Benjamin Mandelkern, *Escape from the Nazis*, Lorimer, 1989. Years ago, when I was writer-in-residence in a Toronto library, Ben Mandelkern brought me a short, true story about surviving, as a Jew, the Nazi occupation of Poland. I was so impressed I suggested he write more, and Mandelkern returned the next week with the manuscript for this book, a story which he had begun to write several years before. Much of the European texture of Mandelkern's voice was removed from the published version, but it's a gripping, first-person memoir of the Holocaust.

Brian Maracle, *Back on the Rez: Finding the Way Home*, Viking, 1996. A journal and meditation by an urban Mohawk in search of his identity. An authentic voice, but Maracle is constrained by the diplomacy of writing about his own family and community.

John Bentley Mays, *In the Jaws of the Black Dogs*, Penguin. An unusual and powerful confessional about suffering from chronic depression. Mays is also an opinionated art critic and writes well about cityscapes in the *Globe and Mail*.

The Diary of Anaïs Nin, 1931-1966, The Swallow Press and Harcourt, Brace & World. There are seven volumes and various editions of Nin's famous diary. Her story varies according to what edition you read. In my mind, this diary defines the contemporary form.

The Diary of Samuel Pepys. Pepys carefully preserved his diary, but it wasn't published for more than a century after his death. A model for everyone who keeps a journal.

Charles Taylor, *Six Journeys*, Anansi. As much criticism as biography, Taylor's portraits are an exploration of the Canadian soul.

Margaret Trudeau, *Beyond Reason*, Paddington Press, 1979, and *Consequences*, Seal, 1982. Sensational confessions when they were published in 1979 and 1982, these memoirs by the estranged wife of prime minister Pierre Trudeau still reveal more about the psychology and culture of the time than Pierre's own dull *Memoirs* (McClelland & Stewart).

Essays of E. B. White, HarperCollins, 1977. A good writer to learn from, but not to imitate. White's best pig story is his children's book *Charlotte's Web*.

The best sources for life writing are small magazines, especially those published by collectives to reach target, minority audiences. You should be able to find these magazines in public libraries or large bookstores. Mass-market women's magazines such as *Homemaker's* also publish life stories – Penny Williams is a regular contributor to *Homemaker's*. Steer clear of the theoretical, analytical books. The whole point of life writing is spontaneity.

CHAPTER 7

The Journey in Real Time

THE TRAVEL STORY

Travelling from one place to another is the most literal and obvious kind of journey. A travel story offers a ready-made plot, opportunities for adventure, scenic marvels, and, if all goes well, encounters with entertaining and unusual people. The problem is deciding where to go. Is there any place left that has not been colonized by McDonald's, CNN, or Disney?

I am not talking about tourism. Tourism stories feature theme parks, Caribbean cruises, and castles in Scotland, and they are intended for people who want to travel with all the comforts of home. Travel stories are for people *who don't want to leave home*. A good travel story is so unique and satisfying that any attempt to replicate the journey is impossible, and to visit the place itself would destroy the illusion. Do I really want to ride a camel to Swat? Paddle down the Amazon? Sail the Pacific Ocean on a raft? Thanks, no.

Some of the best travel stories are fiction. I am thinking of Chaucer's *Canterbury Tales*, the works of Rudyard Kipling, Joseph Conrad, Ernest Hemingway, and Graham Greene, Thomas Mann's "Death in Venice," Robert Louis Stevenson's *Treasure Island*, and

E. M. Forster's *A Passage to India*. A typical travel story, true or imagined, involves a struggle with adversity – storms, blizzards, bandits, bureaucrats, disease – and a clash of cultural values: East/ West, aboriginal/white, primitive/civilized, good/evil.

Cultures, including our own, are subject to a multiplicity of ambiguous interpretations, and these values change over time. It's hard to write a travel story these days without following in somebody's footsteps, but be careful that the path you choose is not booby-trapped with racial, religious, or political stereotypes.

Examine your own cultural baggage. Who are you? Where are you going, and why? Travel writers don't have to have a motive other than curiosity, but without a purpose and a destination, a journey can turn into a pointless ramble. Travellers, even armchair ones, tend to be suspicious of foreigners and easily bored. As a dependable guide, it's the writer's job to keep the reader alert and impatient for the next bend in the road, without being bossy, misinformed, or garrulous.

To enhance their authority, and calm the fears of their hosts, adventurers often adopt the pose of scientific investigators. The British have been particularly adroit at the busywork of collecting specimens, keeping notes, measuring buildings, making drawings, and taking photographs to disguise their true identities as explorers, soldiers of fortune, dilettantes, or spies. The writing may have been a secondary motive, or a means to an end, but the works of T. E. Lawrence, John Ruskin, and Sir Richard Burton have helped define travel literature and given it a gloss of erudition.

Genuine scientists can also write wonderful travel stories, although they are condemned as "popularizers" by their less literary colleagues. In the early years of the twentieth century, anthropologist Vilhjálmur Stefánsson's accounts of his adventures with the Eskimo not only made him famous, but revolutionized our attitudes about the Arctic. Stefánsson's success was later emulated by Norwegian scholar Thor Heyerdahl, who used his voyages in his raft, *Kon-Tiki*, and papyrus boat, *Ra*, to demonstrate the possibilities of prehistoric intercontinental population movements. Heyerdahl became an inspiration for the literature of environmentalism, and for an endless stream of stories about sailing around the world in small, dangerous craft.

Some parts of the world – India, Russia, China, the Middle East – never lose their fascination for North American writers. A mythic quality enhances a country's appeal for readers, and simply because others have gone before is no reason to stay home. Three recent books about Israel, all by professional Canadian writers, illustrate how a familiar topic can be approached in different ways.

In *The Garden and the Gun* (Lester & Orpen Dennys, 1988), Erna Paris adopts the role of Intrepid Reporter anxious to explore Israel's political and moral dilemmas, especially with respect to the plight of the Palestinians in the occupied zone. Paris travels alone to Israel, and structures her narrative around conversations, interviews, and observations. Unlike the average reporter, however, Paris, a secular Jew, is on a personal quest to reconcile her family's painful memories of the Holocaust with Israel's military violence, and it is her vision of the Israeli Jew as victim/victor that gives her book its critical and emotional edge.

Mordecai Richler, on the other hand, travels to Israel as the Famous Author. *This Year in Jerusalem* (Knopf Canada, 1994) presents Israel as a backdrop for Richler's musings about his boyhood chums in Montreal, anecdotes gleaned from gossip, and political opinions derived from *The Jerusalem Post*. He never strays far from his hotel or taxi, insists on a good lunch, and keeps a weather eye out for a bar. Richler, who is travelling with his wife, never makes clear his purpose in going to Israel, and he becomes impatient with Israelis who do not share his views. Richler writes about himself; Jerusalem is a prop.

The *pukka sahib* school of travel writing – "You boy, fetch the bearers!" – is a popular legacy of colonialism. We enjoy reading about the obscenely rich as well as the naked poor, and by adopting a manner of aristocratic reserve, writers can compare the "high life" of their own class with the "low life" around them. These writers' experiences are also conditioned by the fact they have money, and most of the people they meet want to get their hands on it. It's a relationship that tends to give travel stories a skewed view of human nature.

Male writers, for instance, like to visit communes, brothels, and other places where sex is free or cheap. It's not surprising that in these stories women generally fall into the low-life category, or that a lot of weird babes can be found in strange places. The dippy hippie and strung-out chick from Noo Yawk have become such stock characters that I suspect the guys are stealing from each other's stories. Women have difficulty dealing with the world's underbelly without getting raped or murdered, but nineteenth-century British gentlewomen Susanna Moodie and Anna Jameson had a sharp eye for the shortcomings of the Irish, Yankees, and backwoods Canadians.

In *My Jerusalem: Secular Adventures in the Holy City* (Doubleday, 1994), Bronwyn Drainie proves that a domestic role need not interfere with a good travel story. Drainie spent two years in Israel as the wife of a newspaper reporter and the mother of two young boys. She had an opportunity to get to know her neighbours as equals, and by concealing the fact that she was half-Jewish, she gained access to the homes of orthodox Israelis who shunned secular Jews. As an Irish Canadian unbeliever, Drainie also suffered ostracism and verbal abuse.

My Jerusalem is a classic fish-out-of-water story. Like Moodie (*Roughing it in the Bush*, McClelland & Stewart, 1962), Drainie is concerned with household crises, and she turns them into parables illustrating the vicissitudes of Israeli life. She has time to visit and sightsee, and her eye for colour, architecture, and incident makes her an entertaining companion. Drainie explores the Arab and Christian as well as Hebrew aspects of Jerusalem, and because she rarely shirks an argument, even if it means a fight, she exposes the emotions behind the taboos and prejudices she encounters. Like all good writers, Drainie has the ability to remember conversation and record it later as it was spoken. Her opinions are forthright, at the risk of giving offence, but, as she points out, the Israelis are very rude.

Israel is a popular location because it's ancient, complex, and dangerous. A travel story demands personal risk – the possibility of being frozen to death, kidnapped, or killed – and hundreds of journalists are jailed, tortured, and murdered every year. Danger intimidates a lot of writers, including me. Maybe that's why one of my favourite books is Don Starkell and Charles Wilkins's *Paddle to the Amazon: The Ultimate 12,000-Mile Canoe Adventure* (McClelland & Stewart, 1987).

Starkell is an adventurer in the tradition of North America's great voyageurs. In 1980, Don, age forty-eight, and his two sons, Dana and Jeff, launched their twenty-one-foot fibreglass canoe on the Red River in their home city of Winnipeg, Manitoba. Two years later, Don and Dana – Jeff had returned home – arrived at the mouth of the Amazon River in Belém, Brazil. Don writes in his introduction:

> We have taken some 20 million paddle strokes to get here and have travelled every variety of waterway. We have slept on beaches, in jungles, in fields – sometimes in the canoe, on the open water. We have shared simple food and lodgings with the Cuna Indians, the Guajiras, and the Miskitos; we have

dined aboard million-dollar yachts. We have eaten shark, turtle, paca, tapir, wild pig, manioca, palm hearts, cactus. In Cartagena, we ate heaps of roasted ants. We have encountered hundreds of species of creatures: snakes, crocodiles, piranhas, morays, sharks, whales, bees, and scorpions. Strangely enough, the only animal that has given us any trouble was man; we have been arrested, shot at, robbed, jailed, and set upon by pirates. At one point we were led off at gunpoint to be executed. We have been taken for spies and saboteurs, have capsized 15 times at sea and spent terrifying nights in pitch blackness riding the ocean breakers without navigation. We have had brushes with the drug trade, suffered food poisoning, blood poisoning, and dehydration. Forty-five times our canoe has been broken on rocks or reefs. Our skin has been baked to scab by the sun. We have been close to starvation.

Paddle to the Amazon has more than enough terrifying and creepy incidents to give readers shivers of delight, but it's Don's personality and emotional reactions that make these incidents significant. Here's how he describes their arrival at Alvarado on the Gulf of Mexico:

The seas were rough, and as we reached the jetty at the mouth of the river, the swells, which had been just manageable until then, were magnified by the action of the shallows, and by the current of the river which drains hundreds of square miles of tidal lagoon. At this point the tide was on the way out. Suddenly, a 15-foot wave rose to our left. In a fury of spray and confusion, it picked us up and flung us through the air, upside down, into the sea. My first concern was for Dana, but, on surfacing, I saw him beside the canoe about 15 feet away. Fortunately the canoe cover had stayed on, keeping our equipment in place. "Just keep cool," I shouted. "Hang on, and the waves will carry us in!"

How wrong I was. Within seconds, we were being carried out to sea by the powerful current from the river. "Stay cool!" I kept calling, but privately I was beginning to panic, as the waves flipped us around. For the first time in my paddling career, there was nothing I could imagine doing to help myself or my crew – in that current swimming was impossible, and there was no way we could have paddled the canoe full of water. All the while, as we clung to the gunwales, this deadly current was carrying us further from shore. We were certain the fishing boats at the mouth had seen us swamp, but none of them was on its way to help.

Further out we went, as I continued to call to Dana, urging him to be calm.

In spite of their physical danger – they were eventually rescued by a trawler – Don's concern and affection for his son make this passage memorable. We share his terror and feeling of helplessness, we hear his anxious voice calling in the vast expanse of sea. Dana is silent, as he is for most of the narrative. His relationship with his father was often strained to the breaking point, and the tension between father and son adds a deeper psychological dimension to the narrative. *Paddle to the Amazon* is a "trip" in the most existential sense of the word, a test of two men's courage, stamina, and love.

All travel stories demand interesting companions. James Boswell spent years cajoling Samuel Johnson to accompany him on a walking tour of Scotland, and Johnson's witty and outrageous remarks made Boswell's *Journal of a Tour to the Hebrides with Samuel Johnson, LLD*, 1785, an instant popular classic.

A travel writer has to be flexible enough to take advantage of found opportunities, and bold enough to engage strangers in conversation. In *Empire of the Soul: Some Journeys in India* (Stoddart), Paul William Roberts not only seeks out hermits, holy men, and opium smugglers, but makes the most of chance encounters. In Goa, he discovers that a basilica is displaying the four-hundred-year-old body of St. Francis Xavier. Unable to resist, Roberts joins the line of pilgrims shuffling past the glass case:

> The "incorruptible body," I noticed, was somewhat less incorruptible than it had been back in 1554. It was almost entirely draped in worn, dusty, ancient and elaborate robes, like those a pope might wear on special occasions, only the head, feet and one hand visible. His entire right arm seemed to be thrust out of sight behind his back. And these parts were barely more than a skeleton covered with what resembled the skin of an incredibly old and desiccated prune. They lay in a violently vulgar gold casket. Saint Francis must have had dreadful dental problems. Besides being the colour of a chain-smoker's, his teeth were so chipped he could have been chewing on the Rock of Ages with them. Next to the saint's display case was another, much smaller one. Scarcely larger than a shoe box, it contained what looked like the petrified feces of some small creature. I asked the seedy, well-fed cleric who had cheerfully taken our rupees what the objects in the second case actually were.
>
> "They are toes of the Saint Francis," he answered.
>
> "Toes?"
>
> "Correct."

"Why are his toes not attached to his feet? If you don't
mind me asking."
"They are being bitten off by a nun."
"A nun?"
"A nun in an ecstatic state."

A simple question, a brilliant story. (Roberts goes on to tell us
that a nun *did* bite off the toes, and a pope made off with the saint's
right arm.) This brief exchange of dialogue also captures the pecu-
liar charm of Indian English, and contrasts it with Roberts's
clipped, sceptical British voice.

Roberts's sense of humour, coupled with empathy and humility,
enables him to handle the extreme frustration and discomfort of
travelling in India without adopting the sneering tone of revulsion
common to travellers in impoverished countries. Here is part of
Roberts's account of a day-long trip on a hot, filthy, overcrowded
rural bus.

An hour later we had stopped five times to pick up a few
more farmyards, two Tamil nuns, and a woman with an
arse like a sofa. She made her way belligerently down the
aisle, then lowered herself beside the man next to me. Soon
she'd squeezed him practically into my lap, sighing mightily.
She carried a huge plastic holdall, much repaired and reinforced with various kinds of string. From this she pulled a
kerosene pressure stove, giving its brass torso a good pump,
then placing it by her feet *and actually lighting it.* Adjusting
the roaring bracelet of flame, to her satisfaction, she next
produced an old aluminium saucepan tied in a cloth to hold
its lid on. She unwrapped this, peered beneath the lid at
what smelled like stewed moss in tamarind gravy, and finally

placed it on the sputtering blue fire below. These exertions required that she angrily shift three hundred pounds of buttock until she'd achieved the extra room she needed for her culinary work. I was half out the window by now, and the little man had drawn his feet up and was perched on two square inches, like a squirrel, with his chin resting on his knees. The heat and smell from the kerosene stove grew unbearable.

"This is ridiculous!" I told the woman finally. "You can't cook a bloody meal on a bus. It's dangerous. It's probably against the law, too. Why didn't you bring a packed lunch?"

I felt like John Cleese in *Fawlty Towers*.

The woman gave me an evil, uncomprehending glare and went on unpacking a pile of chappatis, a stainless steel container of lime pickles, and another of homemade yogurt. Then she bent to stir her pot with an absurdly small teaspoon, releasing a mighty fart as she did so.

"Jesuschristalmighty!" I exclaimed loudly, appealing to the other passengers for support.

No one knew remotely what I was going on about. Some even looked as if they wished they'd brought stoves along, too, glancing enviously at the steaming pot. Indians are punctual and fussy eaters, incapable of missing a proper meal. They are also deeply suspicious of food cooked by others.

The old man beside me did not seem in the least bit bothered by any of this. He continued to puff on beedies, staring blankly at the untamed expanse of scrub, rocks, and steep hills passing by, its color increasingly bleached by a climbing sun that was almost white behind the veil of dust usurping air and sky.

But Roberts hasn't finished his story yet.

I reminded myself that someday all this would seem merely funny. And I had to admire the woman's ability to set up an entire kitchen and dining table in what little space she could steal on a moving bus, without spilling a drop of anything or setting herself on fire. Within fifteen minutes, the stove was out and she was serving herself fresh hot vegetable curry with warm chappatis, sliced mango, pickles, and yogurt. The size of her prodigious lap came in handy. Nestled in the folds of her sari, every container had its place, and she seemed no less comfortable on a moving bus than if she were sitting at a restaurant table.

Then she spooned a selection of this ingenious meal onto a chappati and offered it to me. She fed the little old man, too, and we all munched away hungrily. Hoping she'd not understood a word I'd said during her cooking, I fished out some plantains I'd bought in Bangalore and divided them among us. All of a sudden, three strangers had become three friends having a picnic.

This anecdote is a story in microcosm. It has conflict and resolution, scraps of speech, drama, momentum, emotion, well-defined characters (I have omitted many of Roberts's details) and imagery that engages our senses. Placing the cooking operation in the context of Indian eating habits adds to our knowledge: the curry is vegetable, the pickles lime, the yogurt homemade.

Roberts has a masterful command of English, and his Innocent Abroad approach conceals his prodigious scholarship. *Empire of the Soul* is based on numerous trips to India over twenty years, and it is as much a work of history as the story of one man's adventures.

Roberts's erudition sometimes intrudes on his narrative, but historical context gives meaning to places and practices that would otherwise be incomprehensible.

HISTORY: THE JOURNEY BACK IN TIME

Centuries ago, history was sung by poets and musicians. Their stories had to be crowd pleasers, so they usually sang about battles and romance, kings, gold, and evil monsters. Then, once we started to write things down, history became the property of the caste that could read and write: the scribes and scholars. History disappeared into the university, where storytelling was replaced by an emphasis on research that became increasingly obscure and irrelevant to contemporary life.

We still tend to assume that history can only be written by academics. One reason is logistics: university teachers have the time and financial resources to devote years to the meticulous digging and sifting historical research requires. A few academic historians can transform their research into superb stories; some refuse because they fear distorting the facts, or prize obscurity, and others fail because their prose is polluted by jargon, or they haven't a clue how to go about structuring a story.

Academic history, however, is only a small, specialized fragment of the voluminous historical literature that has been published in North America in the past forty years. History has become demystified as more and more students attend university, use libraries, and learn research skills. Inspired by E. L. Doctorow and Gore Vidal, writers have rediscovered the historical novel. Margaret Atwood, the author of a true crime novel, *Alias Grace* (McClelland & Stewart, 1996), wrote an early poem about Susanna

Moodie, and Michael Ondaatje, who uses real characters in his fiction, has published a book of poems about Billy the Kid. In 1967, Canada's centennial celebration inspired thousands of community and institutional histories written by amateurs, a trend that is still going strong: the first book I wrote was a pictorial history of the sugar beet industry in Manitoba.

We have also seen a successful marriage between history and journalism. A postwar generation of university-educated newspaper reporters saw the historical roots in the news they reported, and they understood that today's news is tomorrow's history. Okay then, why not write history *as if it were news?*

The writer who made this breakthrough was Pierre Berton with his first book, *Klondike: The Last Great Gold Rush, 1896–1899* (McClelland & Stewart), published in 1958. Berton, a Vancouver reporter, had grown up in the Yukon – his father was a failed prospector – and as a child in Dawson City his imagination had been fired by gold rush lore. *Klondike* grew out of Berton's personal experience:

> I used to wade in the shallow waters of Bonanza Creek and, in the winter, drive my dog up the hard-packed snow of the Klondike Valley road. As children we played steamboat in the relics of some of the old stern-wheelers rotting in the boneyard across the river. Around me were the relics of the early days, human and inanimate: old saloons, dance halls, and gambling houses, creaky and vacant, crammed with Klondike bric-a-brac – old seltzer bottles and tarnished gold-scales; stacks of gold pans long disused and rusty; the occasional satin slipper, worm-eaten; chipped mahogany bars, glasses, beds, armchairs, hand organs, porcelain chamber pots, spittoons.

Berton wanted to write something more ambitious than a childhood memoir or family history, and he wasn't put off by the fact that over one hundred books had already been published about the Klondike gold rush. On reading them, he found them obsolete, incomplete, and, in most cases, wrong. "One of the great problems in putting the story together was to separate fact from fiction," Berton writes in an afterword. "I have followed the rule of trusting more to contemporary first-hand witnesses than to later memoirs, and of cross-checking all dubious statements against others more reliable. In some cases where I have not been able to resolve conflicting versions of an incident, I have so indicated in the body of the text."

Berton's historical methodology is impeccable, but he was not content with archival sources. A journalist needs to get to the *real thing*:

> I have crossed the White Pass half a dozen times by rail and have been down the Yukon River by small boat, steamboat, and airplane. I have covered the whole of the Mackenzie route from Edmonton to the delta by boat and plane, and most of the Peace River and interior British Columbia routes as well. I have travelled the Alaska Highway for its full length by car and been up and down the Alaska Panhandle several times. I know the creeks of the Klondike and Indian River watersheds almost as well as my backyard.

Having gained a firm grasp of the Klondike's geography, and a wide variety of perspectives, Berton then projects himself back in time, telling his story as if he is describing events as they occur. He makes unabashed use of the sensational newspaper stories published at the time, but his real influence is the television news.

Klondike's scenes are full of action – mobs of people running, squabbling, shrieking, dogs howling, whistles blowing – and Berton's sentences move along at a breakneck clip. He relies heavily on what television people call *visuals* – colourful dress, eccentricities, bizarre behaviour – and this technique is perfectly suited to a story featuring prostitutes and psychopaths, blizzards, fires, and disasters. Berton's description of an avalanche at Sheep Camp illustrates how he transforms a dusty newspaper clipping into a vivid picture, complete with soundtrack.

> The scene was a weird and terrible one. Small air holes sometimes appeared in the snow to mark the spot where a man or woman had been buried, and somewhere beneath them the searchers could still hear the muffled cries of the victims. Those who still lived beneath the snow (and only a few had been killed by the slide) could hear one another talking, and conversations were carried on between them. Relatives above called out their last good-byes to those entombed below. One old man could be heard alternately praying and cursing until his voice was stilled. But even the strongest could not move a muscle, for the snow was packed around them as tightly as cement.
>
> As the hours wore on, those who were not rescued at once slowly became anesthetized by the carbon dioxide given off by their own breathing; they began to feel drowsy, and drifted off into a dreamless sleep from which few awoke. Their corpses were lifted out in the days that followed, many of them still in a running position, as if forever fleeing from the onrushing avalanche.

Klondike's immense critical and commercial success inspired Berton to write more histories, and persuaded other journalists to follow. *Klondike* also changed readers' attitudes about what history is. It legitimized the use of newspapers, interviews, and personal memory, and encouraged the writer to take an active role in shaping the story. Gone was the myth of objectivity, and with it the historian's godlike role as judge of human affairs.

Berton also wrote about ordinary people, grubby people, and Canadians saw themselves in the characters he portrayed. History is us! *Klondike* democratized the writing of history, opening it up to everyone who had been excluded. Since almost everyone had been excluded, almost everybody is writing about it. History now includes stories that are part memoir and biography, documentary, political analysis, diatribe, drawings, photographs, statistics, interviews, and imaginative reconstruction. Do your own thing, but *get it right.*

ORAL HISTORY

The invention of the cheap cassette-tape recorder helped restore history to its oral tradition and, since even the very old can recall no more than eighty or ninety years, it shortened the time frame of what we consider to be the past. Studs Terkel in the United States and Barry Broadfoot in Canada produced oral histories of the Great Depression, *Hard Times* (Pantheon, 1970) and *Ten Lost Years* (Doubleday, 1973) respectively, barely thirty years after the depression ended.

Oral history established the contemporary personal interview as a legitimate source for history and biography, and gave a voice to the common man, but as Pierre Berton points out, memory is unreliable. Recollections tend to be distorted and sentimental, and a lot of very bad history is based on old wives' tales.

Oral history can be boring. I hate reading transcripts of taped interviews masquerading as stories. The questions are usually sycophantic, the answers banal. Serving up raw meat is lazy journalism. The writer may disappear altogether, leaving the reader to figure out who's talking and why, and when an oral history is organized thematically, with various people talking about the same topic, interviews are ripped out of time and place. In *Ten Lost Years*, Broadfoot doesn't even identify who is speaking. Has he interviewed a hundred people, or five? Where did he find them? How? What has he edited out? Why? As a writer, I find transcribing and editing tapes a chore. If you want to preserve an authentic encounter, why not make a video?

LOCAL HISTORY

Local history has become so popular that it's hard to imagine a community that doesn't have one. However, you may discover that the existing books are balderdash, and as time passes, events take on new meanings. Local history tends to rely too heavily on uncorroborated reminiscences and family trees, or the writers feel their purpose is to paint a rosy picture of their community. Local historians tend to make the mistake of describing clubs or institutions – the Lions, Women's Institute, the Royal Bank – rather than telling stories about the most interesting *people* in the community's history.

The danger in writing local history, of course, is that you risk offending your neighbours by ignoring some event or organization they feel is important, or by telling stories they'd rather not see published. It's almost impossible to include everything and still have an exciting story. However, there's no need to write about something simply because it happened. Keep the dustbin of history close at hand. Use it, but don't toss out the good stuff.

SOCIAL HISTORY

If you look beyond your own community, as Berton did, you will be able to see it as part of a larger tapestry. For instance, I recently discovered in a local history, *Early Settlements of King Township, Ontario*, that my village, King City, is located on the first railway line built in Ontario. That line, the Northern, which linked Toronto and Aurora in 1853, is still in use, and I listen to the trains hoot as they pass in the night. The book's author, Elizabeth Gillham, noted the railway's construction in passing, but it could have become the entry point, or lead, into a story about life in Canada in the latter half of the nineteenth century.

The railway line was built by a pair of unscrupulous speculators, Sir William Mackenzie and Sir Donald Mann, who amassed great fortunes before going bankrupt, and whose financial misadventures eventually led to the creation of the Canadian National Railway. Mackenzie and Mann, who lived in Toronto, were embroiled in all the social and political intrigues of their era. By placing myself on the map in King City, I connect to a story of national significance full of greed and skullduggery. Maybe I'll write it!

Social history is a rebellion against the convention that history is about Very Important People and Big Events, i.e., kings, politics, and wars. In France, it is the history of the *sans-culottes*; in North America, it is stories about rural, domestic, and family life, women's movements, native people, racial and religious minorities, sex, strikes, commerce, fashion, disease, and natural disasters. I like to think of it as "found" history, stories woven from chance encounters or everyday objects that take on significance beyond themselves. For instance, the discovery of bundles of old letters in the attic of a house she'd bought in Kingston, Ontario, prompted Merilyn Simonds to write *The Convict Lover* (Macfarlane Walter &

Ross, 1996), the true story of a love affair, by correspondence, between the young woman who had lived in the house and a prisoner in Kingston penitentiary.

Unearthing letters, diaries, memoirs, or photographs may trigger an exciting paper chase if you can find memorabilia left by people who knew each other, or who were involved in the same events. In *The Private Capital: Ambition and Love in the Age of Macdonald and Laurier* (McClelland & Stewart, 1984), Sandra Gwyn relies on the handwritten diaries of a nineteenth-century civil servant in Ottawa, Edmund Meredith, supplemented by unpublished reminiscences by his wife, Fanny, and son, Coly. Fanny, a member of Toronto's old, prominent, and controversial Jarvis family, gives Gwyn an entry into the secretive, incestuous world of colonial Victorian "society," and Meredith, a sociable gossip, provides a cat's-eye view of the machinations of Ottawa politics and hijinks of visiting British aristocrats.

Gwyn soon discovered that in Ottawa, everybody not only knew each other, they wrote to, and about, each other, and considered their letters and diaries important enough to donate to archives, particularly the National Archives of Canada, where they became public property. They also enjoyed having their pictures taken – exchanging photographs was equivalent to handing out business cards today – and vied fiercely for recognition in the social columns of newspapers and magazines.

It was a series of these columns by "Amaryllis" in *Saturday Night* magazine that gave Gwyn her point of entry into *The Private Capital.* "What fascinated me," Gwyn writes in her preface, "was that this pseudonymous, turn-of-the-century journalist seemed to be a kindred spirit; I could relate immediately to the way she wrote about Ottawa. What interested Amaryllis all those years ago was precisely what had always interested me as a magazine writer: not so much the flow of political events as the *texture* of those events – how people actually live and behave as opposed to the specifics of what they actually accomplish."

Borrowing from true crime, Gwyn set out to unravel the mystery of Amaryllis's identity, and her search, guided by Amaryllis's sly, perceptive columns, provides the thread that leads us through a complex period of history spanning more than forty-five years. *The Private Capital* has plenty of texture – Gwyn devotes a whole chapter to sewage – and its feminine/feminist perspective gives her a perfect excuse to discuss courtship and marriage, childbirth, illness, scandal, and other aspects of our lives academic historians, most of whom are male, ignore.

Events can also be entry points for social history. Numerous books have been written about the Rebellion of 1837 and the Winnipeg General Strike in 1919, which proves that interest in events does not necessarily diminish with time. Prohibition inspired James Gray's *Booze* (Macmillan Canada), a story of rum-running on the prairies, and its Ontario counterpart, *The Rumrunners* by C. H. Gervais (Firefly). Gray relies heavily on newspaper accounts, government reports, and his own memories; Gervais emphasizes eyewitness interviews and photographs.

Nothing is too offbeat or mundane for social history. Margaret Visser's *Much Depends on Dinner* (McClelland & Stewart) is about eating; other writers have chronicled the history of hair and of hanging. Themes may be serious – deportations and concentration camps – or entertaining: Alberto Manguel has written a *History of Reading* (Knopf Canada). Many business books, especially those about frauds and stock market crashes, are social histories, and so are some analytical books such as David K. Foot's *Boom, Bust and Echo* (Macfarlane Walter & Ross, 1996).

The intimidating thing about social history is its scope. What am I going to do with all these people? How can I cope with five hundred years? What do I choose? How do I process tons of research material? Where does it all end?

Once you find the right entry point, one thing should lead to another: a diary will suggest a newspaper obituary, which mentions the names of other people, whose memoirs you find in the library, which has books full of photographs, and so on and on. If this doesn't happen, you're starting in the wrong place. What is your found object? An ideal entry point has a jolt of recognition – Eureka, I've got it! – that gives shape and impetus to your story.

Follow your thread where it leads, but remember that you are weaving on a loom with a solid frame. How are you going to tie your threads together so they won't unravel? Who are your central characters? Why? Will your readers be excited, shocked, or titillated? Do you have a plot? Is there point and purpose to your story?

As the threads multiply and a pattern emerges, snip off the loose ends. Be ruthless. Get rid of people and events who have nothing to contribute to your story, however important they may be, or have been, in real life. Resist the urge to dash off on fascinating tangents: a story about rum-running could easily expand to include the histories of whisky, organized crime, the Ontario Provincial Police, and the temperance movement, as well as biographies of the Seagram and Bronfman families, Nellie McClung, and Al Capone.

Once begun, where will you end? Death is always convenient. It can be the death of an individual, a class, or an era – look at all the books written about the Great War. Death gives a satisfying feeling of completion to your story; it finishes a cycle which begins again. History eventually becomes a journey in present time.

FAMILY HISTORY

When it comes to writing what we want to know, an amazing number of people want to know about their ancestors. A family tree can easily grow into a thick book that includes anecdotes and interviews, or it may provide enough material for a narrative by a family member. Family histories are usually intended for the family alone, but in some cases, as I'll show later, they are good enough to be published as trade books.

Family history research, or genealogy, has evolved from a snobbish hobby into an international subculture. In Canada alone, there is a vast network of clubs and societies, newsletters, Web sites, conferences, videos, compact discs, and guidebooks full of advice. So much new research is published every year that you may be able to trace your roots with surprising ease.

A few years ago, for example, I was talking casually with a man I had just met, Philip Jackson. He began to tell me his family legend: his great-grandfather, John Jackson, had been the illegitimate son of a British lord and a parlour maid. Hey, I thought, that's *my* family legend, except in my mother's version it had been a kitchen maid. As I puzzled over the coincidence, I remembered that though my mother was born in Saskatchewan, her grandmother had been a Jackson from near Sarnia, Ontario. In Sarnia, with Philip's help, I found a history of the Leckie family, which told me that Jane Leckie had married John Jackson in 1845, and my great-grandmother, Ellen, was one of their daughters. Philip and I are cousins. (The Leckie family history does not identify John Jackson's parents.)

Our shared story illustrates two essential points Angus Baxter makes in his indispensable guidebook, *In Search of Your Canadian Roots* (Macmillan Canada, 1994). "*Never* believe anything you are told about your family unless it can be proved," Baxter warns, and, in particular, "stories of royal or noble descent should always be very suspect." Drat. As Baxter points out, humble families tend to embellish their social status, and most of us in North America come from humble families.

Begin your research with your own family. Try to locate old photographs, marriage records (and divorce decrees), land titles, letters, diaries, and scrapbooks. Relatives may have saved documents they have forgotten about, and you may find a treasure trove of memorabilia stored in an attic or a trunk. Interview the oldest members of your family. Where were they born? What date? When and where were they married? What dates were their children born, and where? What were their parents' names? Grandparents? Where were they born? When did they die? Where? How many children did they have? And so on.

Take notes, and press for precise answers. Learning that great-grandmother Eliza was born in Dartmouth, Nova Scotia, is a lot more help than being told she came to Alberta from "down east." Try to get full names. My mother, for instance, had been named Margaret Ellen after her two grandmothers. Remember too that Eliza is Elizabeth, and can be Beth, Lizzie, Betty, Bessie, or Lisa. As a girl, my great-grandmother Ellen was called Nellie, and Margaret can be shortened to Peggy. My father, Henry, was always known as Harry. Someone named John may prefer to call himself Jack, Jake, Sean, or Ian.

You will need correct names to confirm your information by searching official records, especially if you come from one of those extended families where several generations of cousins are named "William" or "Mary." The correct spelling of surnames is also important. Has a family name been changed, shortened, or simplified? A name such as Brown, for instance, could once have been Braun or Bronstein.

Your questions are simple, but getting answers may be frustrating. Memories are faulty, and if people don't know the answer, they may invent one that seems plausible. Speak to all of your relatives – the least likely sources may turn out to be the best – and ask all of them the same questions. You may find contradictions, or uncover information others have forgotten or suppressed. Don't be upset or discouraged if you encounter indifference, evasiveness, or hostility.

Says Baxter: "You must be prepared to find that no one in your family shares your interest in ancestry. You will meet with comments like 'Leave well enough alone' or 'Why stir the pot?' or 'The less you know about them the better.' Often these remarks hide fear or taboo knowledge. Some may be afraid you will discover some dark secret, or they may know the secret."

Once you have wrung everything you can from your family, the next step is to check the accuracy of this information and gather more. This stage demands time, patience, and money. Expect to write letters, make long-distance calls, and travel to archives, churches and graveyards in North America, or much farther afield as the tree takes shape. Invest in a computer to organize your information and in the technology to communicate by e-mail.

Begin with your public library. It may have a genealogical department, or someone on staff who can help you find the sources you need. If your ancestors lived in the area, the library may have a local history that mentions them, as well as maps, atlases, land records, and microfilm copies of old newspapers. It can also put you in touch with libraries in other communities, and you can borrow all kinds of material from them on interlibrary loan. The library will know if there is a local historical or genealogical society, and should be able to provide addresses and phone numbers for regional and provincial archives.

The family history department of the National Archives of Canada (395 Wellington St., Ottawa, ON, K1A 0N3, Tel. (613) 995-5138) publishes a free forty-eight-page booklet, *Tracing Your Ancestors in Canada*, and welcomes all inquiries. Baxter's book, *In Search of Your Canadian Roots*, contains detailed listings of archives, libraries, genealogical societies, and church records for every province, including addresses and phone numbers. The greatest virtue of this book is Baxter's critical assessment of all these resources. You will have to do a lot of running around, so there's no need to waste time barking up the wrong tree.

Try to find a friendly archivist who will help you locate records, explain what they mean, and answer your questions (see Chapter 2). Establish personal contact by phone, fax, or e-mail, especially if it's not convenient for you to visit the archive in person. Outline your project and ask for assistance. An archivist might do some sleuthing on your behalf or locate sources you hadn't thought of. Expert help will prevent mistakes and misinterpretations and may save you days, even years, of fruitless labour. You will also learn more quickly how to find your own way through the maze of indexes, directories, census returns, cemetery records, and court documents.

The hardest part is reading microfilm. I hate it, but it's unavoidable. Family history is not for anyone who lacks the stamina to crouch for hours over a cranky machine that is always going out of focus or out of order. The drudgery can be discouraging, but these dry old records have tales to tell. A census will record the number of cows and horses your pioneer ancestors owned, how much of their land was cleared, and whether they could afford a wagon. If you are puzzling over a family secret, you may find a will that says "to my adopted daughter, Jane," or that leaves Jane out altogether. Obituaries can be full of news, and you might discover from an old newspaper that great-great-grampa shot himself or absconded with the church funds.

Family history research can go on forever. When do you stop? Remember, history is a story. It should have a plot, or a theme, and be interesting to someone other than yourself. Unless you believe in eternal life, establishing kinship with the dead is significant only if they have stories attached to them. I could probably trace my lineage to "Fat Duncan," the Scottish king murdered by Macbeth, but how much do I care about all the Duncans in between?

You may come up with a story that will knock your family on its ear, but even sketchy or mundane material can be enhanced by the way you present it. Rather than organizing events chronologically, you may want to start in the present by telling the story of your search, or begin with the most dramatic event in the family's history. Choose one or two characters to be your focal point. Arrange the others around them. You can write yourself into the story, or tell it from your own point of view. This may irritate your distant relatives (who are the Leckies, anyway?), but hell, you've done the work.

Do not lie, launder, or worry about defaming the dead (see Chapter 10). Do not present your family as a bunch of plaster saints. Change pace and voice by quoting from documents, or by inserting photocopies. Include photographs if they have a story to tell. Consult and quote from history books to place your family in time and space. What sort of community did they live in? Who else was there? What were the economic conditions? Was there class strife, religious argument, or racial tension?

Let's look at how a family history can grow into a successful narrative. The first passages I have chosen come from *The Surprise of My Life* (Wilfrid Laurier University Press, 1998), a memoir and family history that Claire Drainie Taylor, widow of Canadian actor John Drainie, originally wrote for her grandchildren.

Her manuscript begins:

The Place: a small farm a few kilometres outside a village in Southern Russia – the year around 1870. The doctor fills out the death certificate for Anne Rosen – three-year-old victim of the current plague. As he drives off in his horsedrawn buggy, he assures the bereaved young parents that Jewish tradition will be observed: he will send the death-wagon for the child's body in time to have her buried before sundown of the following day. He disappears in the falling snow which develops into a raging blizzard before he reaches the village. Three days pass before the hearse can make its way through the windswept snowdrifts to the farm. On the morning of the second day the child, Anne, wakens and asks for a drink of water.

Having escaped being buried alive, Anne recovered, grew to young girlhood and eventually, in the company of her parents, five sisters and two brothers, emigrated to Canada where the family settled in and around Winnipeg, Manitoba.

With a few simple, well-chosen words, Drainie Taylor tells a dramatic story, describes her ancestral home, establishes her Jewish identity, and moves her family to Canada. She also draws attention to a key person in her story – Anne Rosen – and uses the present tense to make the past more immediate.

The Surprise of My Life is Drainie Taylor's first venture into prose narrative, and she began writing it when she was over seventy. As a storyteller, she has some advantages – a background in radio drama and a tempestuous marriage to a cultural icon – but she deliberately avoids the limelight-and-celebrities formula. *The Surprise of My Life* is a domestic chronicle shaped by her traditional roles as daughter and granddaughter, wife, lover, mother and grandmother, and it tells us a great deal about the lives of middle-class Canadian women during the twentieth century. It is the kind of story any woman might write – if she has the courage to make her private life public.

"It made me very, very sad and frightened," she writes of a period when she felt her marriage to John Drainie was crumbling.

> I couldn't handle the bizarre double life we were leading. I had had about as much as I could take of the carousing, drunken arguments and sleepless nights. And I was terribly worried about the children hearing and not understanding what all the screaming and shouting was about. When John and his pals got completely out of hand I'd just go up to bed, enraged and despondent. I could never quiet them down – they never listened to me anyway.

> John generally came up to bed around 3 or 4 a.m. Oddly enough, he didn't collapse in a drunken stupor. Alcohol is said to diminish one's libido: not John's. Many times he'd reach out for me and I, despite my anger with him, would respond to his touch. After all those years he was very familiar with my erogenous zones and I think it gratified me to have hate sex instead of love sex; it can be very challenging and exciting. Try it sometime.

> (I am assuming my grandchild who is reading this is old enough to empathize with my feelings. If not, you shouldn't be reading it!) When we'd waken in the morning, all passion spent, the chill between us might continue or, depending on the circumstances with the children, we might be friendly. I mean, it was hard to stay mad if we woke to find little bodies snuggled in our bed, or, as on one memorable occasion,

Jossie's little body and three cats in a neat row all tucked up to their chins lying peacefully between us.

Drainie Taylor accomplishes many things in these brief passages. By confronting her own unhappy memories and ambivalent feelings, she gets back at John, exposing him as a heavy drinker with crude friends and a violent temper. She winks at her grandchildren, a signal that her family has weathered the crisis, yet her image of Jossie and the cats suggests that the children *had* been frightened.

Events are not significant unless they affect us. How do your family members relate to each other? What is your family scenario? What roles have people played, and why? Can you find in your family research a common thread, a dynamic that explains their behaviour or psychology? Will your relatives discuss their fears and failures, their motives and differences of opinion? Will you reveal yours?

Build your narrative on the three milestones of birth, marriage, and death, but emphasize unusual or traumatic events that run counter to convention. Painless childbirth, happy marriage, and peaceful "passing away" will not grab your grandchildren's attention. Choose incidents, even small ones, that reveal conflict and character. Claire and John Drainie returned from a disappointing honeymoon to find John's mother waiting for them in their living room.

"I was wretchedly embarrassed," Claire writes.

In fact, we all were. John kissed his mother. I just stood there – speechless.

Mrs. Drainie had come down to check on the apartment, she explained, and to welcome us with fresh daffodils from her garden. At that, I found my voice and thanked her

profusely, but immediately lost it again. Nobody knew what
to do. I should have offered to make tea, but I was completely
nonplussed by the situation. Besides I didn't feel that it was
my apartment – she was more familiar with it than I was. And
I didn't really know her but I knew she didn't like me and that
she disapproved of our marriage. What was I to do? I waited
for John to give me a lead but he must have felt the same
tenseness because he, too, was unable to come up with anything. So Mrs. Drainie finally said, "Well, I don't suppose you
want me here any longer."

And over our half-hearted protestations, she left. We stood
together at the door calling and waving "goodbye." She never
turned around. She just kept walking down that long narrow
corridor – the saddest looking woman in the world. All these
years later, I can still see her – that lonely figure in the grey
felt hat, grey tweed coat and sensible shoes trying not to let
us see that her heart was breaking.

The confrontation couldn't have lasted more than a few
moments, but this passage runs a gamut of conflicting emotions,
all fraught with sexual tension. Drainie Taylor heightens the
tension by using contrast – yellow daffodils and grey hat and coat
– and by dropping Mother Drainie's hurtful remark into a pool
of silence.

Bring your family to life by describing their appearance, pos-
sessions, and quirks of behaviour. Don't rely on photographs.
Colours fade, or change. Black-and-white photos may suggest
skin colour, but not the colour of hair or eyes. Everybody appears
to wear black, although their clothes may have been red or blue.
Photographs tend to be posed, and they often make people appear
bigger than they are. People dress up, or remove their glasses. I
would never have guessed from photographs, or from hearing his

voice on the radio, that John Drainie limped, and photos of United States president Franklin Roosevelt artfully concealed that his legs were paralyzed. When I saw a dress once worn by suffragette Nellie McClung on display at a costume museum in Dugald, Manitoba, I was astonished to realize that McClung had been barely five feet tall.

Write a precise physical description of all your family members, including your own generation and your children. Describe their houses, furniture, cars, taste in food and drink. Don't write "beer" when it's Coors, or "soft drink" if it's Diet Pepsi. Things which seem obvious to you today will be exotic to your descendants. Capture personality. It may be a voice, a laugh, a pattern of speech. If your ancestry is Cree, Irish, or Jamaican, your relatives will speak English in different ways, and the strength of their stories is in the telling.

An old hat, a walking stick, a pocket watch, or a few pieces of heirloom jewellery will give you clues about your family's style and the society in which they lived. Much can be made of a pack of cards, a battered pair of skates, a boat rotting on the shoreline. Don't forget what has been thrown out. As a child, I sometimes helped my Grandmother Duncan lace herself into her corset, her "stays" as she called them, and felt a party to torture. Nammy's corset is long gone, yet now, decades after I burned my last girdle, I realize that she was strapping on her armour, and I, her faithful page, was learning the ropes.

Finding answers to your first questions will suggest more probing questions about interests, behaviour, and values. Did your ancestors paint or play an instrument, hunt, knit, or chew tobacco? How did they get along? There are few families without a feud or a falling out, divorce, estrangement, or rivalry. If someone tells you "Bert was a mean old bastard," ask why. You need evidence to give your story credibility, and the remark may be motivated by malice.

Never accept gossip as fact, or reject it as lies. You will have to authenticate and evaluate your information, and use good judgement about the weight you give it.

Okay, you have collected all these characters, events, and anecdotes spanning perhaps several hundred years. How do you shape this amorphous material into a coherent story?

A simple and effective device is a journey back to your ancestral home. It is a multiple journey through space, time, and memory, and it allows you to locate your ancestors along the way. You may be a chatty, opinionated tour guide and use "I" a lot, or you can pretend to be a video reporter and talk to the reader as your memories return.

What *is* your ancestral home? Your decision will be based on family myth and nostalgia. You may choose your descent from your mother, as many families do, or from the most romantic, famous, or tragic figure in your story. The home could be the place where you were born, or a village a member of your family lived in centuries ago. By choosing your destination, you determine your story line.

Travel alone, or with a sympathetic companion, and be prepared to spend time (a pit stop on a tour bus is worse than useless). Your long-lost relatives may be hostile or indifferent, if you find them. Don't forget they've been sitting on your history all the years you've been away. You will probably not share their values, or even their language, and you may dislike each other.

If this happens don't pack your bags and head for the airport. Their view of your family may be diametrically opposed to yours, but that doesn't mean that one is right and the other wrong. Avoid arguments. Ask questions and respect their answers. You may get an entirely new slant on your story, and a clash of cultures and personalities will make it more exciting.

The journey model works beautifully for Denise Chong in *The Concubine's Children: Portrait of a Family Divided* (Viking, 1994). A westernized, second-generation Canadian economist, Chong did not intend to write a family history when she went to China in 1985 with her companion, television journalist Roger Smith. As a child, she had been scared of her eccentric grandmother, Leong May-ying, and troubled by her mother, Winnie's, stories of growing up in gambling dens and sleazy hotels as May-ying's only Canadian daughter. May-ying had taken her two older daughters, Ping and Nan, to China. Nan had died, and Winnie had not heard from Ping in nearly forty years.

"It was passing faces in the crowds in China that stirred awake a curiosity from my early childhood," Chong writes. "The photograph of the two young girls, my mother's two sisters, that lay among the pile in the cedar chest kept coming to mind. A feeling that I had to stand on the same soil dogged me. I didn't know why I wanted to, only that I could not leave China without going to the village of my grandfather's birth. I also knew that Mother had to accompany me. Persuading her was the hard part."

Winnie had no sentimental attachment to China and ambivalent feelings about meeting her Chinese family for the first time. Curiosity, however, got the better of her, and Denise arranged transportation for the two of them in a Chinese government van. Word of their arrival had gone ahead, and when they arrived in the village the first person to greet them was Winnie's half-brother, Yuen. All Winnie knew about Yuen was that he had been born with club feet.

"We heard him before we saw him," Chong writes.

The rhythmical slow, sweeping sounds were the footsteps of a thin man, clad in dark blue baggy cotton. As he limped into the room, both his feet looked to be on backwards, like a broken doll whose legs had twisted around and stuck.

"Elder Sister," he said, nodding to Mother.

"*Ah* Yuen," Mother said as she rose and embraced her brother, feeling the sorrow of his crippled feet but also the joy that they swept away any doubt that he was an imposter. "How did you know who I was?" she asked. "I recognized your face," he said. Yuen had a face that reflected the quiet strength and squareness of my grandfather's. "*Baba* sent photographs."

Out in the dirt courtyard, as we were taking our leave of the officials to go to Yuen's house, a woman in baggy pants and layers of cotton blouses appeared. The quickness of her movements, the proud lines of her face and her girlish smile were my grandmother reincarnated. Mother hugged her sister, Ping, for the first time. Through tears, both sisters fumbled for photographs.

This encounter inspired Chong to research and write *The Concubine's Children*, but she places the reunion appropriately at the *end* of her book. She begins with an earlier voyage:

> In a small village in China, the concubine, pregnant, consults a blind fortune teller, whose predictions are considered to come closer to the truth than those of a sighted one. He tells her that the child she is carrying is a boy. A concubine is supposed to produce sons; Leong May-ying has failed her husband, Chan Sam, twice already. She decides this long-awaited son should be born not in China but in Canada, the land the Chinese know as "Gold Mountain." The predicted son, the one who came to Canada in the womb and whose stay was bargained for a house in China, was my mother.

The ironic opening expertly establishes the central theme of duality and conflict: China/Canada, wife/concubine, son/daughter, wealth/poverty. It introduces May-ying, explains her status, and suggests that she is superstitious, manipulative, mercenary, and unlucky. I am hooked. I want to know more about Mayying, the house in China, and her unexpected, unwanted daughter. Chong has anticipated my need. She writes: "Fifty years after Mother's father, my grandfather, built his house in the village of Chang Gar Bin in Kwangtung province in south China, Mother and I stood in its front reception room. It was spring of 1987." With a quick edit, Chong sets me down in the house with her mother and introduces herself. Ping and Yuen have something they want to return to their sister, and Yuen motions them to follow him upstairs.

At the top of the stairs was a vast floor space, interrupted by three beds, each shrouded in mosquito netting. Yuen led us to the far corner into a small room. In the decaying wood of the screens that enclosed the room, gouge marks were still faintly evident where decorative porcelain panels had been lifted out. Ping intoned: "This was supposed to have been a room for guests. *Baba* said that he wanted a place to entertain friends and relatives, a place to sip tea together." Like her brother, she never missed an opportunity to pay homage to the grandeur their father had intended when he built this house. To Mother and me, the room looked to be a storeroom. It held an inventory of junk: a tall, rusting metal crib with broken springs, crockery topped with split corks, an RCA Victor phonograph that had probably been silent for decades, an assortment of cracked straw baskets.

Yuen rummaged around and finally handed Mother a faded bundle of brown cloth. The bundle, shook out, fell into the shape of a coat, a child's perhaps. With sure hands, Mother reached slowly for the collar, found its black velvet trim. She threaded her arms through the sleeves and drew the coat over her shoulders, exposing elbows and wrists that betrayed when she had last worn it. But the ill fit fell away when she pulled the sides of the collar together to wrap her neck in velvet. It was as if the coat, in its last performance, in forbearance and forgiveness, had itself restored the two halves of the family – one in Canada, one in China – to one.

Mother had been a girl when she'd last worn it. With its velvet trim and chamois lining, the brown bouclé knit coat had been a rare extravagance of her mother's. She had purchased it on Vancouver's fashionable Granville Street, several blocks from Chinatown where the two of them lived. Mother had paraded Vancouver's sidewalks in it, arm-in-arm with her girlfriends. Never had she guessed it would live out its life in China, that her mother had given it to her father to include in one of his regular care packages to his other family there.

Ping had sashayed along the village paths in it, enjoying the taunts of the other villagers: *Faan-gwei neu*. The coat that labelled her "the foreign girl" had passed from her to Yuen, and when he outgrew it, it had been kept in safekeeping for more than forty years, away from looting Japanese soldiers, Communist vigilantes, and the moths of time, stored along with Ping and Yuen's hopes that Mother, their sister, was still alive in Canada.

The coat is an eloquent symbol, but it is the *discovering*, the stair climbing, rummaging, shaking out and trying on, that engages me. I can see all their anxious, expectant faces, hear fragments of their muted conversation, the long silences, the glad outpouring of reminiscences. I hear Denise's annoyance in the word "intoned." Elder Sister Ping is staking her claim to the family house, and while Ping has worn and cherished her Younger Sister's cast-off coat, she makes it plain that Winnie will always be a "foreign girl."

Having framed her story between a family legend and an eyewitness report, Chong begins her historical narrative with a photograph.

May-ying traced a part down the back of her head, bound the hair on each side with a filament of black wire and twisted it into a chignon above each ear. Then she unpinned and combed the curls framing her forehead. She assessed the finished look in the mirror: a girl of seventeen looked in; the reflection was supposed to pass for a woman of twenty-four.

It had been Auntie's advice to wear her hair up to add years to her face. May-ying set her dangling earrings swaying. The earrings, along with a jade pendant, had been her mother's; she had taken them off to give to her child when they'd said goodbye forever. As long as she had her jade and gold near, the souls of her ancestors would do all they could to keep harm from her path.

She stood up, turned away from the mirror, smoothed the *cheong sam* over her girl's body and went to sit for her portrait as the wife of a man she had not yet met.

Chong has invented this scene by studying May-ying's portrait, which she reproduces later in the book. Dramatization adds motion and vitality to the faded photograph and encourages us to see events from May-ying's point of view. The earrings tell their own poignant story, and the mirror image adds a whiff of intrigue. Why does May-ying have to look older? Why has she never met Chan Sam? Who is Auntie? What happened to her mother? In television talk, this scene is called a teaser.

A less imaginative writer might have written the scene this way: "Chan Sam had requested a photograph of seventeen-year-old May-ying so he would recognize his concubine when she got off the ship in Vancouver. He had bought her from Auntie for more than two thousand dollars. Chan Sam had a wife in China, but Canadian law forbade Chinese men to bring their wives and families into the country. May-ying had little say in the matter. When she was about four years old, her parents had sold her to Auntie, a stranger, as a servant. Her earrings were a parting gift from her mother. Because May-ying would be travelling on a false Canadian passport, she put up her hair to look old enough to match her assumed identity."

Chong uses active verbs and clear, descriptive language. She builds her anecdote around her most startling piece of information, but reveals it near the end. She ends her anecdote with a kicker, an unexpected twist that makes us want to know more about May-ying's mystery husband.

Not many of us have a concubine for a grandmother, but a scandalous past doesn't necessarily make a story. Canada's Chinatowns were full of young women like May-ying who worked as waitresses and prostitutes in tea houses and mah-jongg parlours. May-ying stands out because Chong portrays her as a heroine in the mould of Bizet's Carmen or Scarlett O'Hara in *Gone With the Wind*: beautiful, temperamental, and independent. Chan Sam, an inept Micawber with two wives, grandiose ideas, and impeccably bad timing, could have stepped out of a Charlie Chaplin film.

The Concubine's Children began as oral history when Chong was about five years old. "I became curious about what Mother was like when she was my age," she writes. "I was fascinated by the differences between the little girl she'd been and who I was. Mother would talk, I would listen. I remember laying out a sewing pattern with Mother when she told me how she'd had to fetch the stick she was disciplined with. Her pen traced the path on the tissue paper. As Mother's pen went back and forth, tearing the tissue to shreds, she relived her terror, and so did I."

Chong didn't perceive the historical importance of her mother's stories until May-ying and Chan Sam had been dead for years. "To recover the family's past in Canada," she writes, "I had to rely upon my mother's memory. What she first spilled was a mud puddle of emotion. Only with discipline and patience did she and I begin to order the past. The very nature of the old Chinatowns – the poverty, the lack of education, the claustrophobic existence – lent itself to a legacy of oral history. Most of Chinatown's inhabitants had only 'chat' to pass the time, and consequently their stories, enlivened by vivid accounts of conversations, were repeated again and again. What my mother overheard of her parents' stories formed some of her earliest memories."

Winnie's own story is one of double identity: when she started school, a teacher insisted she change her Chinese name, Hing, to an English one. She was educated in both Chinese and English, and her ability to tell stories in dialogue with Chinese inflection gives *The Concubine's Children* an authentic Chinese-Canadian sound. One of Winnie's earliest recollections was of going with her father to fetch her mother home from a gambling den.

Chan Sam whispered in his daughter's ear and pushed her forward. "*Mama*? Come home," Hing said. Everyone turned at the child's voice; children were not seen in such places.

Once they were behind the door of their rooms, it was May-ying who had the first say. "I don't need anybody to look after me!"

"Bull-lo-shit! People who go into gambling dens do not think of the future!" he said angrily. "Go in there and you will sink into vice. What do you want gamblers' company for, all that smoking and drinking?"

The Concubine's Children is also the story of Winnie's psychic journey of reconciliation. By going to China, and by remembering, Winnie was able to come to terms with a family history she had found humiliating and a culture she had suppressed. "What she saw and heard in China illuminated her own past," says Denise. "Instead of making her bitter, it lifted the burden of her shame."

Family history has been one of the pillars of western literature since Homer wrote *The Iliad*. Sophocles' *Oedipus Rex* is family history. So are Shakespeare's tragedies, Tolstoy's *War and Peace*, Eugene O'Neill's *A Long Day's Journey into Night* and Joy Kogawa's *Obasan*. Both *The Concubine's Children* and *The Surprise of My Life* are structured around familiar literary devices – a lost sister, a harrowing death, marital conflict, sexual jealousy, rage and reconciliation.

Your voyage must have a goal, every anecdote a point. Please do not tell us everything you know about your family – your story will read like one of those letters some people circulate at Christmas. Eliminate the irrelevant (you can include a family tree if you like) and don't include events simply because they happened. Try to see your ancestors' lives through their eyes, and avoid imposing your own values. Let the facts speak for themselves – a gravestone can be very eloquent. And if your family is truly boring, write about someone else's.

FURTHER READING

Irving Abella and Harold Troper, *None Is Too Many*, Lester & Orpen Dennys, 1982. A devastating exposé of Canadian anti-Semitism before and after the Second World War. Superb history.

Angus Baxter, *In Search of Your European Roots* and *In Search of Your British and Irish Roots*, Macmillan Canada. Essential for researchers looking beyond North America.

Family History News, an excellent, user-friendly quarterly newsletter published by Parr's Publishing, Oshawa, ON, L1G 5R4.

W. H. Graham, *Greenbank*, Broadview Press, 1988. A definitive local history of the rural area in Ontario where Graham lived when he wrote it. Graham's research dispels any myths about the "good old days" back on the farm.

James Gray, *The Winter Years*, Macmillan Canada, 1966. A memoir that is also a social history of the Depression in Winnipeg. Gray has written many lively books about the prairies.

Thor Heyerdahl, *The Kon-Tiki Expedition* and *The Ra Expedition*, Doubleday. These are the most famous and dangerous of Heyerdahl's many adventures.

Michael Ignatieff, *The Russian Album*, Penguin, 1988. The drama of Ignatieff's story of Czarist Russia is heightened by his economy with words and calm, reflective tone.

Anna Brownell Jameson, *Winter Studies and Summer Rambles in Canada*, New Canadian Library, McClelland & Stewart, 1990. A lively, astute, and critical look at Upper Canada in the year before the 1837 Rebellion. For women travellers, Jameson set a model of fearlessness.

Alan Moorehead, *The White Nile*, Hamish Hamilton, 1960. A masterpiece of historical travel writing.

Rona Murray, *Journey Back to Pesharwar*, Sono Nis, 1994. One of the best of the return-to-the-Raj books.

Michael Ondaatje, *Running in the Family*, McClelland & Stewart, 1982. Part travel book and memoir, *Running in the Family* is precise, concise, sad and hilarious. Here are the seeds of all of Ondaatje's poetry and fiction.

Don Starkell, *Paddle to the Arctic*, McClelland & Stewart, 1995. This trip nearly cost Starkell his life. There is a whole subgenre of recent travel books about the Arctic.

Vilhjálmur Stefánsson, *My Life with the Eskimo*, Collier. First published by Macmillan in 1913, this is a prototype in the Great White Hunter school of exploration literature. Stefánsson became more famous as a writer than a scholar. His reckless slaughter of wild animals would not be popular today.

Sylvia Van Kirk, *Many Tender Ties: Women in Fur Trade Society, 1670–1870*, Watson & Dwyer, 1980. Beautifully told stories about the aboriginal women who became the wives and partners of the fur traders.

Ronald Wright, *Time Among the Maya*, Penguin, 1989. Wright is erudite, and his straightforward, conversational manner is remarkable for its lack of egoism.

CHAPTER 8

The Journey in Present Time

Many stories are stories-in-progress. They have begun, but the writer may not yet know the outcome. In the case of crime stories, the writer may know the ending, but enhances the suspense by concealing information until the end. Many newspaper stories are stories-in-progress. The writer drops in on a person or event, writes a story, then does follow-up stories as things unfold. Often the stories add up to a book. Election campaigns are the most obvious example of unfolding stories, and they have spawned a sub-literature of boys-on-the-bus books that relive each campaign, minute by minute, as if it were still going on.

Present time is an illusion. When journalists write in the present tense, they are fooling us into thinking "I am there." In his 1970 essay "Radical Chic," Tom Wolfe uses present time to create a fly-on-the-wall view of a cocktail party conductor Leonard Bernstein had thrown some weeks earlier for the Black Panthers.

The Field Marshal of the Black Panther Party has been sitting in a chair between the piano and the wall. He rises up; he has the hard-rock look, all right; he is a big tall man with brown skin and an Afro and a goatee and a black turtleneck much like Lenny's, and he stands up beside the piano, next to Lenny's million-dollar *chatchka* flotilla of family photographs. In fact, there is a certain perfection as the first Black Panther rises within a Park Avenue living room to lay the Panthers' ten-point program on New York Society in the Age of Radical Chic. Cox is silhouetted – well, about nineteen feet behind him is a white silk shade with an Empire scallop over one of the windows overlooking Park Avenue. Or maybe it isn't silk, but a Jack Lenor Larsen mercerized cotton, something like that, lustrous but more subtle than silk. The whole image, the white shade and the Negro by the piano silhouetted against it, is framed by a pair of bottle-green velvet curtains, pulled back.

The casual immediacy of this scene disguises Wolfe's careful framing – after all, he'd just invented the phrase "radical chic" – and conceals the weight of research and social criticism behind his observations. I suspect Wolfe cruised the room later, peering at the photographs, stroking the curtains, and turning over the china and silver to look at the trademarks (good reporters do this). The black-and-white contrast is emphasized by the repeated use of "silhouetted."

Wolfe's tone is slightly incredulous, as if he has no idea what will happen next. He is saying: "Here I am in this room, but can I really believe what I am seeing with my own eyes?" Of course he knows how the evening turns out, but he is allowing the reader to *experience* the party through his own observant, rather superior sensibility:

Suddenly, before Don Cox can open his mouth, Lenny reaches up from out of the depths of the easy chair and hands him a mint. There it is, rising up on the tips of his fingers, a mint. It is what is known as a puffed mint, an after-dinner mint, of the sort that suddenly appears on the table in little silver Marthinsen bowls, as if deposited by the mint fairy, along with the coffee, but before the ladies leave the room, a mint so small, fragile, angel-white, and melt-crazed that you have to pick it up with the tips of your forefinger and thumb lest it get its thing on a straightaway, namely, one tiny sweet salivary peppermint melt . . . in mid-air, so to speak . . . just so . . . Cox takes the mint and stares at Bernstein with a strange Plexiglas gaze . . . This little man sitting down around his kneecaps with his Groovy gear and love beads on . . .

Wolfe called this style of writing "the new journalism," and it was hot stuff, especially in New York City, during the 1970s. Its strengths were attention to detail (Wolfe had checked out the mint bowl), a feeling of perpetual motion – the mint rises on Bernstein's fingertips and seems to hang in the air before Cox takes it – confrontation, and reversed roles: Wolfe portrays the Panthers as groovier than the Manhattan socialites.

I remember being blown away by "Radical Chic" when I read it in 1971. New journalism certainly influenced me and many journalists of Wolfe's generation, but when I reread "Radical Chic" twenty-five years later, I found the tone smug and sarcastic.

The problem wasn't just dead slang and Boring Buzzwords, *non sequiturs* and the annoying punctuation that had seemed so iconoclastic at the time. It was arrogance. Wolfe pinpoints it himself in his introduction to his anthology *The New Journalism* (Harper & Row), published at the crest of the wave: "The idea was to give the full objective description, plus something that readers had always had to go to novels and short stories for: namely, the subjective or emotional life of the characters. Eventually I, and others, would be accused of 'entering people's minds' . . . But exactly! I figured that was one more doorbell a reporter had to push."

Norman Mailer pushed it hard with *The Executioner's Song* (Little, Brown, 1979), a true crime story based on interviews and written in a journalistic style. Mailer, however, called it "a true life novel." A novelist as well as a journalist, Mailer understood when he was imagining, or surmising, his characters' emotions and thoughts. No matter how long a journalist spends on a story, no matter how close we get to our subjects, or how probing the questions we ask, we can never presume to know what is going on in other people's heads beyond what they tell us, and that's suspect. Even body language may suggest something quite different from the truth.

The only minds most New Journalists succeeded in entering were their own, and since they were almost all white, male Americans, they tended to be preoccupied with the usual topics: women, crime, sport, cars, power, and money. It was the same old stuff, with attitude. In retrospect, the *new* journalism was being written by women, and published in magazines such as *Ms*, *Chatelaine*, *Maclean's*, and *Cosmopolitan*. Women's viewpoints were so provocative the writers didn't have to go Gonzo.

DOCUMENTARY NARRATIVE

Wolfe's "I am here" style of writing used to be called *reportage*. Reportage is now an obscure word, and because this kind of journalism has been influenced by film, radio, and television, I call it documentary narrative.

Print journalism began to develop a descriptive, on-the-spot style when writers had to compete with movie newsreels and live radio broadcasts. It became okay to reproduce chunks of dialogue as it was spoken, rather than filtering the story through an omniscient narrator, and for a writer to call the plays like Foster Hewitt on "Hockey Night in Canada." (Sports reporting still has some of the manic quality of early radio.) Television showed writers how to add colour and detail, change points of view, and use a variety of wide-angle, zoom, and close-up shots. Wolfe, for instance, sets up the Black Panther with an establishing shot, then zooms in on the mint.

As a writer, however, Wolfe is able to bring more to the scene than a camera could show. He tells us how the mint smells, feels, and tastes, traces its origin to the Marthinsen silver bowl, and transforms it into a symbol of culture clash. He uses the incident to slow the tempo of his story, and does his little minty riff to build anticipation. In other words, Wolfe, like a magician, shows us only what he wants us to see. If your documentary is heavy on detail for its own sake, or includes far more information than the reader needs to know, it will collapse under the weight of irrelevance.

A documentary style can give the illusion of present time even when it is written in the past tense, and writers rely on it to give vitality to a story which lacks action. For example, a book about an elderly, housebound woman dying slowly of cancer seems, at first glance, unpromising. However, in *Twelve Weeks in Spring* (Lester & Orpen Dennys, 1986), June Callwood transforms the last weeks of Margaret Frazer's life into a day-by-day drama featuring Frazer's encounters with her multitude of caregivers, including her doctor, Linda Rapson, and Callwood herself:

> That evening Margaret for the first time allowed me to spoon-feed her. Her dinner consisted of a few mouthfuls of mushroom soup, without the mushrooms, and some ice cream mixed to a puddle with maple syrup. With long rests between, I put tiny amounts in her mouth with the smallest silver spoon I could find to spare her the effort of opening her mouth wide.

Margaret seemed distracted and distant. I pushed the coffee table out of the way and pulled up the rocking chair so I could sit beside her and hold both her hands in mine. She said, "Linda thinks that I will . . . that there's more of a chance that I will die than get well. What do you think?"

I said carefully, "It doesn't look good, but who knows?"

Margaret received this with an indifferent nod, as confirmation of old news. Then she lay back on the pillows and looked out of the bay window at sunlight sifting through her maple trees. Suddenly she turned to me, eyes blazing, and cried out, "I'm not going to die!"

I said, "Yes you are. But no one knows when."

She closed her eyes. I held her hands tightly and watched her slow, exhausted breathing. I began to cry. Tears rolled down my cheeks and my nose dripped. I didn't want her to hear me sniffle and I didn't have a hand free to get a tissue out of my pocket. As I was struggling for control, she sensed what was happening. She opened her eyes and looked at me with a fathomless gaze.

"I don't want you to die," I explained helplessly.

There was nothing more to say. She simply closed her eyes again and, after a moment, I let go one of her hands and wiped my nose and wet face.

Callwood's careful attention to detail elevates the simple act of spoon-feeding to an important event, and rather than telling us how she feels, or imagining how Margaret feels, she allows actions, words, tears, and silences to speak for themselves. Callwood, a participant as well as an observer, emphasizes the conflict in the scene – Margaret could be an opinionated and cranky patient – and expresses emotion through the simple gesture of wiping her nose and wet face.

Callwood visited Frazer for a few hours once a week, but in *Twelve Weeks in Spring* she creates the illusion that she was on the spot every hour of every day. Here is Callwood's depiction of the earlier conversation with Rapson that had upset Margaret:

> When Linda made her Wednesday house call, Margaret demanded an explanation for feeling so weak.
>
> "Does it mean I won't get better?"
>
> Linda looked at her. "I don't think it is likely that you will," she said quietly. "Your chances are very slim."
>
> Margaret was shocked, which surprised Linda. It was clear that Margaret had believed that she could postpone her death for months. Margaret protested hotly, "But I *want* to get better! I'm trying to get better! I really thought that I was improving."
>
> They ate lunch together, talked idly of flowers and birds, and listened to music. Though Margaret seemed calm, Linda was worried and reluctant to leave. She offered to brush Margaret's hair, and Margaret instructed her where the brush could be found upstairs in her bedroom. Linda had fetched it and was trying to subdue Margaret's stiff white hair when someone knocked at the front door and entered the house, calling, "Yoo hoo." It was Laura Legge.

Callwood was nowhere near, but by interviewing Rapson, Legge, and all the other caregivers, who rotated on a twenty-four-hour shift basis, Callwood is able to recreate moods, thoughts, and conversation. She also relies on the entries team members made in a daily log, and makes the most of homely activities – preparing food, weeding the garden, getting Margaret up and down stairs, friends coming and going, and, most of all, talk. Dialogue makes her story lively and moves it along at a brisk pace, and when she feels it necessary, Callwood provides her own witty commentary on people and events.

Other documentary writers choose to remain invisible, use quotes sparingly, conceal the mechanisms of their research and maintain a cool, dispassionate tone. This authoritative approach works well for broad, serious themes, such as political and social analysis, that require the writer to shape an amorphous mass of material into a coherent narrative. Highlighting significant dates in present time – the "day-in-the-life-of" technique – gives the writer a series of pegs to carry a heavy load of historical background, biographical data, and interpretation.

Transitions between present and past can be indicated by leaving a space between paragraphs, or simply by starting a new paragraph or chapter. Don't switch too often – the reader will get time-warped – and don't use present time unless something actually *happens*.

Documentary narrative is a flexible, experimental form that can encompass every kind of contemporary story from investigative reporting to social history and political criticism. It has become so omnipresent that when people talk about "non-fiction," the documentary form is usually what they have in mind.

THE DIARY OF SAMUEL PEPYS

Pepys's diary is so difficult to categorize, and it has had such a seminal influence on journalism, it deserves an entry to itself. Samuel Pepys (pronounced peeps), a diligent and ambitious young secretary to the earl of Sandwich, kept a daily journal of his life in London for nearly ten tumultuous years, 1660 to 1669. During this time, Pepys, whose errands brought him in close contact with the court of King Charles II, met the king's mistresses, observed the ravages of the Black Death, and witnessed the Great Fire of London. Although Pepys's monumental manuscript, first published in 1825, is called a diary, it is a masterpiece of documentary narrative.

Pepys was not introspective. He was too busy, inquisitive, and pleased with himself to brood. On July 6, 1661, he writes:

> Waked this morning with news, brought to me by a messenger on purpose, that my uncle Robert is dead; so I rose sorry in some respect, glad in my expectations in another respect. We rode, and got well by nine o'clock to Brampton. My uncle's corps in a coffin standing upon joynt-stooles in the chimney in the hall; but it begun to smell, and so I caused it to be set forth in the yard all night, and watched by my aunt. My father and I lay together to-night, I greedy to see the will, but did not aske to see it till to-morrow.

Pepys's sang-froid, coupled with his bluntness and curiosity, makes him an acute observer. On October 13, 1660, he writes: "I went out to Charing Cross, to see Major-General Harrison hanged, drawn and quartered; which was done there, he looking as cheerful as any man could do in that condition. He was presently cut down, and his head and heart shown to the people, at which there was great shouts of joy." The next day Pepys has a different adventure:

> To White Hall chapel, where one Dr. Crofts made an indifferent sermon, and after it an anthem, ill sung, which made the King laugh. Here I also observed how the Duke of York and Mrs. Palmer did talk to one another very wantonly through the hangings that parts the King's closet where the ladies sit.

Pepys is cheeky and irreverent, self-effacing but knowing, both tolerant and critical. Nothing is too high or lowly for his gaze. He writes as attentively about plays, dinner parties, and the cost of his wife's lace petticoats as he does about court politics and the plague:

> Captain Ferrers carried me the first time that ever I saw any gaming house, to one, entering into Lincolne's-Inn-Fields, at the end of Bell Yard, where strange the folly of men to lay and lose so much money, and very glad I was to see the manner of a gamester's life, which I see is very miserable, and poor, and unmanly. And thence he took me to a dancing schoole in Fleet Streete, where we saw a company of pretty girles dance, but I do not in myself like to have young girls exposed to so much vanity. So to the Wardrobe, where I found my Lady [Sandwich] had agreed upon a lace for my wife at 6 pounds which I seemed much glad of that it was no more, though in my mind I think it too much, and I pray God to keep me so to order myself, and my wife's expences, that no inconvenience in purse or honour follow thus my prodigality.

This entry reveals as much about Pepys's own moral ambivalence – he tends to inflict his repressed puritanism on his wife – as it does about Restoration London. Pepys did more than simply note the highlights of his day, he passed judgement on them:

> My poor wife rose by five o'clock in the morning, before day, and went to market and bought fowles and many other things for dinner, with which I was highly pleased. By the by comes Dr. Clerke and his lady, his sister, and a she-cosen, and Mr. Pierce and his wife, which was all my guests. I had for them, after oysters, at first course, a hash of rabbits and lamb, and a rare chine of beef. Next, a great dish of roasted fowle,

cost me about 30s., and a tart, and then fruit and cheese. My dinner was noble, and enough. I had my house mighty clean and neat; my room below with a good fire in it; my dining room above; and my wife's a good fire, also. I find my new table very proper, and will hold nine or ten people well, but eight with great room. At supper, had a good sack posset and cold meat, and sent my guests away about ten o'clock at night, both them and myself highly pleased with our management of this day; and indeed their company was very fine, and Mrs. Clerke a very witty, fine lady, though a little conceited and proud. I believe this day's feast will cost me near 5 pounds.

The charm of Pepys's diary, as well as its value as social history, comes from his infallible sense of what was worth writing down. On October 18, 1660, he writes:

This morning, it being expected that Colonel Hacker and Axtell should die, I went to Newgate, but found they were reprieved till to-morrow. The. Turner sent for a pair of doves that my wife had promised her; and because she did not send them in the best cage, she sent them back again with a scornful letter, with which I was angry, but yet pretty well pleased that she was crossed.

19th. This morning my dining room was finished with green serge hanging and gilt leather, which is very handsome. This morning Hacker and Axtell were hanged and quartered, as the rest are. This night I sat up late to make up my accounts ready against to-morrow for my Lord.

Pepys was scrupulous about his sources. When he recorded information he had learned second-hand, he noted it: "I did hear the Queen is much grieved of late at the King's neglecting her, he not having supped once with her this quarter of a year, and almost every night with my Lady Castlemaine, who hath been with him this St. George's feast at Windsor, and come home with him last night; and, which is more, they say is removed as to her bed from her own home to a chamber in White Hall, next to the King's owne; which I am sorry to hear, though I love her much."

Pepys couldn't resist good gossip, but he was careful to distance himself from it, and he often recorded both the name of his informant and the circumstances of their conversation. Pepys was also meticulous about checking facts and numbers, but his greatest asset was his nervous energy. He was incessantly tearing hither and thither, on foot and horseback, by barge and carriage, craning his neck for a better view, listening at keyholes, badgering bystanders with questions. Pepys's diary is a panorama as colourful as a Bruegel painting, and during the excitement of the Great Fire, his breathless voice seems to be speaking aloud, as urgent as if he were in the room. On September 2, 1666, he writes:

Some of our maids sitting up late last night to get things ready against our feast to-day, Jane called us up about three in the morning, to tell us of a great fire they saw in the City. So I rose, and slipped on my night-gown, and went to her window; and thought it to be on the back-side of Marke-lane at the farthest; but, being unused to such fires as followed, I thought it far enough off; and so went to bed again, and to sleep. About seven rose again to dress myself, and there looked out at the window, and saw the fire not so much as it was, and further off. So to my closet to set things to rights, after yesterday's cleaning.

By and by Jane comes and tells me that she hears that above 300 houses have been burned down tonight by the fire we saw, and that it is now burning down all Fish Street, by London Bridge. So I made myself ready presently, and walked to the Tower; and there got up upon one of the high places, Sir J. Robinson's little son going up with me; and there I did see the houses at that end of the bridge all on fire, and an infinite great fire on this and the other side the end of the bridge; which, among other people, did trouble me for poor little Michell and our Sarah on the bridge.

So down, with my heart full of trouble, to the Lieutenant of the Tower, who tells me that it begun this morning in the King's baker's house in Pudding-lane, and that it hath burned down St. Magnus's Church and most part of Fish Street already. So I down to the water-side, and there got a boat, and through bridge, and there saw a lamentable fire. Poor Michell's house, as far as the Old Swan, already burned that way, and the fire running further, that, in a very little time, it got as far as the Steele-yard, while I was there. Every body endeavouring to remove their goods, and flinging into the river, or bringing them into lighters that lay off; poor people staying in their houses as long as till the very fire touched them, and then running into boats, or clambering from one pair of stairs, by the waterside, to another. And, among other things, the poor pigeons, I perceive, were loth to leave their houses, but hovered around the windows and balconys, till they burned their wings, and fell down.

Having staid, and in an hour's time seen the fire rage every way; and nobody, to my sight endeavouring to quench it, but to remove their goods, and leave all to the fire; and, having seen it get as far as the Steele-yard, and the wind mighty high, and driving it into the City; and everything after so long a drought proving combustible, even the very stones of churches; and, among other things, the poor steeple by which pretty Mrs. — lives, and whereof my old schoolfellow Elborough is parson, taken fire at the very top, and there burned till it fell down; I to White Hall, and there up to the King's closet in the Chapel, where people come about me, and I did give them an account dismayed them all, and word was carried in to the King.

So I was called for, and did tell the King and Duke of York what I saw; and that, unless his Majesty did command houses to be pulled down, nothing could stop the fire. They seemed much troubled, and the King commanded me to go to my Lord Mayor from him, and command him to spare no houses, but to pull down before the fire every way. The Duke of York bid me tell him, that if he would have any more soldiers, he shall; and so did my Lord Arlington afterwards, as a great secret.

Here meeting with Captain Cocke, I in his coach, which he lent me, and Creed with me to St. Paul's; and there walked along Watling Street, as well as I could, every creature coming away loaden with goods to save, and, here and there, sick people carried away in beds. Extraordinary good goods carried in carts and on backs.

At last met my Lord Mayor in Canning Street, like a man spent, with a handkerchief about his neck. To the King's message, he cried, like a fainting woman, "Lord! what can I do? I am spent: people will not obey me. I have been pulling down houses; but the fire overtakes us faster than we can do it." That he needed no more soldiers; and that, for himself, he must go and refresh himself, having been up all night. So he left me, and I him, and walked home; seeing people all almost distracted, and no manner of means used to quench the fire.

Pepys's account covers the five days of the fire, and although he was frantic with worry and exhausted from storing his own goods – his house barely escaped – he rarely missed a chance to run out and see what was happening. Pepys' rapid punctuation, incomplete sentences, strategic use of the present tense, shifting points of view, and repeated emphasis on *seeing* prove that he had nothing to learn from a latter-day upstart like Tom Wolfe, although Wolfe seems to have learned a great deal from Pepys.

TRUE CRIME

At first glance, the true crime story appears to be a genre so saturated, competitive, and corrupt it might be wise to avoid it. If the crime is sensational, television networks get to it first, followed by radio talk shows, the daily press, and the tabloids, but if the crime is not sensational, why write about it? Legal prohibitions may make it difficult, or impossible, to write your story before the case comes to trial, and trials can drag on for tedious months. Your research becomes expensive, and you run the risk that the public will become bored, or revolted, before your story is published. You also run the risk of too much competition: half-a-dozen books were published about the Paul Bernardo-Karla Homolka murder case, and even more are in the works, or are already published, about the Bre-X gold mine fraud in Indonesia. Some of these books sell well enough to justify the writer's time and effort, others don't. If you find the turf well staked out, move on.

Readers tend to equate "good" books with books that express "good" values, or at least the values they believe in, and if the crime, or criminal, is too horrific, they may simply choose not to read about it, or demand that the publications be censored. This response is particularly true in the case of stories involving the rape, torture, and murder of children or teenagers. It's odd, because at the same time, readers gobble up horror fiction, and relax by watching movies, videos, plays, and operas depicting the most gruesome violence. Is there something embedded in our psyche that distinguishes between blood and ketchup?

Crime, however, does not equal violence, and a violent crime, however sad or shocking, is not necessarily a story. A man shoots his wife and three children, then kills himself; there are no witnesses, and the story of that troubled family has ended without having been told. A child is starved and tortured to death, but if witnesses turn away as the story unfolds, that child's death is a statistic. Senseless violence is not a story because it's senseless. Where's the motive? Conflict? Character? Plot? These so-called crime stories, ugly slices of life that fill up pages in our newspapers and hours of television time, are nothing more than tearjerkers.

A true crime provides a writer with a ready-made plot and cast of characters, but the story usually lacks a surprise ending. Knowing who dunnit is not necessarily a handicap – we have been going to performances of Shakespeare's *Macbeth* and *Richard III* for hundreds of years – but it means the writer has to emphasize other aspects: motive, psychology, relationships, location, damnation and punishment.

In the United States, death-row stories have been popular since the execution of Julius and Ethel Rosenberg in 1953 following their conviction on charges of espionage. The Rosenberg story resonates because it involved political intrigue, innocent children, a cast of wicked characters, and ambiguities that remain unresolved. It's a contemporary entry in Foxe's *Book of Martyrs*.

Writers in countries that have abolished the death penalty lose the drama of an execution, but they have the advantage of a serial story. Convicted criminals, including killers, are free to write letters, give interviews, and create new stories by being troublesome in jail. Wealthy criminals hire writers. These stories sell. In Ontario and New York state, stories written by convicted thieves, bank robbers, and fugitives became so popular that laws were passed prohibiting convicts from exploiting their crimes for profit. In Canada, this law may soon become nation-wide.

Being a victim of, or a witness to, a crime is an advantage, provided you make it back to tell your story. The literature of victimization is enjoying great popularity, especially in the areas of sexual abuse, child abduction, cults, and institutions run by religious orders (see Chapters 5 and 6). Our definitions of crime are also shifting: racism and sexual harassment are now perceived as crimes, yet suicide, abortion, and revenge by a battered wife are not. Euthanasia is somewhere in between.

Crime stories are culturally defined. Crimes involving prostitutes, drug addicts, and street people are commonplace – crime comes with the territory – but if crime involves the rich, famous, or white middle-class, it's news (unless, as often happens, they succeed in keeping it out of the media). Culture clash plays an important role – witness the O. J. Simpson story, with its echoes of *Othello*. In Canada, crimes and confrontations involving native people continue to provide a rich source of stories, with Indians enjoying their traditional role of villain/victim.

Look for an angle that will make your story unique. Go beyond the criminal/victim axis to the characters around them. Will it help your story, for instance, if your condemned murderer is redeemed by a nun? What role does the judge play? Courtrooms are intimate theatres, and if you hang around during recesses, you'll find that you have a chance to talk to witnesses, spectators, and family members. Police officers are the best gossips I've ever met. Criminal lawyers are often eager to share their information and opinions, and in the tradition of Agatha Christie, your key character may be a detective.

If the police are cooperative, it's possible to write about an unsolved crime. New evidence may have come to light, and a story may jog someone's memory or provoke a witness to come forward. Never write about an unsolved case with which you are personally connected – you will become the prime suspect.

Stories about white-collar crime have a lot of potential, especially when they involve mystery, suicide, and powerful people. Watergate was just the name of a hotel until *Washington Post* reporters Bob Woodward and Carl Bernstein traced a break-in all the way to the White House, and their stories forced the resignation of president Richard Nixon. The discovery of gold in Indonesia by Bre-X Minerals was a business story until a Texas billionaire got involved, and one of the company's geologists jumped, or was pushed, out of a helicopter over the Borneo jungle (oooh, head hunters!). When it was revealed that the geologist had four wives, the Bre-X story turned into a classic tale of sex and death, greed, fraud, corruption, and fool's gold.

White-collar crime stories, however, are complex and time-consuming to research and write, and since the general public is uneducated about business, the market is usually small. The culprits often get off with a slap on the wrist, and regardless of the outcome, nosy writers are threatened, harassed, and intimidated (see Chapter 10). The courts may also be inclined to grant publication bans to influential defendants, even when they are found guilty.

Crime has a moral as well as a legal connotation. A logging company, for instance, may have a legal right to chop down a forest, but environmentalists find it morally intolerable. Environmental stories about clear cutting, pollution, whaling, clubbing seals, and urban sprawl tend to fall into the villain/victim pattern of true crime.

In North America, we ignore the existence of state crime, which numbers its victims in the millions, yet stories will be written about genocide as long as it exists. My vote for the best true crime story ever goes to Aleksandr Solzhenitsyn's *The Gulag Archipelago* (HarperCollins, 1973). An experiment in literary investigation, as Solzhenitsyn calls it, *The Gulag Archipelago* weaves his own memoir of arrest and imprisonment during the Stalinist era into the stories of more than two hundred gulag prisoners, many of whom did not survive the labour camps. Solzhenitsyn goes to great pains to document his evidence, but the strength of the book is his powerful voice, which tempers cold rage with irony and mockery, and finds courage in suffering.

THE POLEMIC

The Gulag Archipelago is an indictment, yet Solzhenitsyn, whose vision of the world is profoundly moral, resists the temptation to sermonize (he succumbs in later work). The sermon, once the most popular form of English narrative, is out of fashion in our sceptical age, but a good rant can still be effective, and fun to write, especially if it's disguised as criticism or satire, lament, requiem, or meditation. The subject doesn't have to be religious. Environmentalist David Suzuki is a polemicist, and so is feminist writer Naomi Wolf. Camille Paglia puts them all to shame. All you need is a firm belief in good and evil, a delight in hellfire language, and a style that booms like apocalyptic thunder.

The literary model was set in the seventeenth century by English poet and cleric John Donne ("Never send to know for whom the bell tolls; it tolls for thee.") Here is an example from Donne's Sermon 76, "On Falling Out of God's Hand."

> That God should let my soul fall out of his hand into a bottomless pit and roll an unremovable stone upon it and leave it to that which it finds there (and it shall find that there which it never imagined till it came thither) and never think more of that soul, never have more to do with it; that of that providence of God that studies the life and preservation of every weed and worm and ant and spider and toad and viper there should never, never any beam flow out upon me ... what brimstone is not amber, what gnashing is not a comfort, what gnawing of the worm is not a tickling, what torment is not a marriage bed to this damnation, to be secluded eternally, eternally, eternally from the sight of God?

Donne, who preached from the pulpit of London's St. Paul's Cathedral, combines phrases that reverberate – "an unremovable stone" – with crisp, plain words – ant, toad, spider – chosen to keep his listeners awake. His imagery – gnashing, gnawing, tickling – made them squirm, and his prose, heavy with its weight of images, swells like a series of waves until the last long breaker – "eternally, eternally, eternally" – crashes against the shore.

Jonathan Swift was also an Anglican cleric, dean of St. Patrick's Cathedral in Dublin, Ireland, and, like Donne, who wrote erotic poetry, Swift took as keen an interest in the present as in the hereafter. Swift's interests, however, were political. He was horrified by the destitution of Ireland's Catholic peasants, and when he found that railing against rapacious absentee landlords from the pulpit did no good, he took a more subtle approach. In 1729, he published a short essay, "A Modest Proposal for preventing the children of poor people in Ireland from being a burden to their parents or country and for making them beneficial to the public."

Swift adopts the pompous, sanctimonious tone of the English gentlemen he loathed, and writes in the pseudo-scientific style fashionable in a society that celebrated rationality. "I am assured by our merchants," he says, "that a boy or a girl before twelve years old is no salable commodity; and even when they come to this age they will not yield above three pounds, or three pounds and a half a crown at most on the Exchange; which cannot turn to account either to the parents or the kingdom, the charge of nutriment and rags having been at least four times that value." Swift then presents the nub of his proposal:

"I have been assured by a very knowing American of my acquaintance in London, that a young healthy child well nursed is at a year old a most delicious, nourishing, and wholesome food, whether stewed, roasted, baked, or boiled; and I make no doubt that it will equally serve in a fricassee or a ragout."

In language that would do a cookbook proud, Swift goes on to make a logical, dispassionate argument for the annual consumption of one hundred thousand Irish infants, professing "to have no other motive than the public good of my country, by advancing our trade, providing for infants, relieving the poor, and giving some pleasure to the rich. I have no children by which I can propose to get a single penny; the youngest being nine years old, and my wife past childbearing."

Satire can accomplish in a brief paragraph what years of sermons will never achieve – it can make people see and laugh at the ghastly truth. Swift turns conventional wisdom on its head by taking a serious problem to its logical, outrageous conclusion. Swift's images are graphic, and his short, compressed sentences cut like sword strokes. You can hear the hiss of his blade in all the words with "s": assured, nursed, stewed, roasted, and fricassee. "Ragout" is aptly regurgitative.

George Grant's *Lament for a Nation* (McClelland & Stewart, 1965) proves the old adage, if you can't make 'em laugh, make 'em cry. Subtitled *The Defeat of Canadian Nationalism*, Grant's lament was as shocking, and prescient, as Swift's proposal, and it is written in a similar cool, laconic style.

"To lament is to cry out at the death or at the dying of something loved," Grant writes. "This lament mourns the end of Canada as a sovereign state. We find ourselves like fish left on the shores of a drying lake."

Canada was preparing to celebrate its centennial anniversary with an orgy of nationalist pride, but Grant's book expressed what many Canadians privately feared, that the "true north strong and free" was a figment of the American imagination. Expressed in calm, elegiac prose, with an edge of bitter irony, Grant's political and economic analysis arrives at an inevitable conclusion: "The confused strivings of politicians, businessmen and civil servants cannot alone account for Canada's collapse. This stems from the very character of the modern era. The aspirations of progress have made Canada redundant. The universal and homogenous state is the pinnacle of political striving."

The cleverness of Grant's lament is that he presupposes a shared loss, and he makes his case as much by creating a mood as through logical argument. Since no one wants to think ill of the dead, Grant evokes a sentimental sympathy for the deceased nation, in spite of the fact that, to all appearances, it seemed to be alive and kicking.

A year after *Lament for a Nation* was published, Pierre Vallières began work on its French-language Québécois counterpart, published in English in 1971 as *White Niggers of America* (McClelland & Stewart). As far as Vallières is concerned, the disappearance of

Canada is good riddance to bad rubbish. He writes: "The author of this book is a Québécois, a French Canadian, a proletarian, a colonized man and a baptized son of the Church. Hence, an extremely frustrated individual for whom 'freedom' is not a metaphysical question but a very concrete problem."

Vallières, steeped in the literature of French nihilism, existentialism, and Marxism, adopted the traditional form of the political manifesto, a call to arms:

> Let us kill Saint John the Baptist! Let us burn the papier-mâché traditions with which they have tried to build a myth around our slavery. Let us learn the pride of being men. Let us vigorously declare our independence. And with our hardy freedom, let us crush the sympathetic or contemptuous paternalism of the politicians, the daddy-bosses and the preachers of defeat and submission. It is no longer time for sterile recriminations but for action. There will be no miracles, but there will be war.

Vallières' politics aside, his book illustrates the polemic's weaknesses as well as its strengths. Vallières gets so bogged down in philosophical analysis and socialist theory his argument trails off into a babble of utopian rhetoric. Rather than trying to convert the sceptical, he preaches to the converted. Many writers make the mistake of yelling at their readers, or think they can persuade by repeating the same arguments over and over. Vallières' political theorizing is unconvincing; his personal story is compelling.

By making part of *White Niggers of America* a memoir, Vallières transforms his repressed, impoverished, alienated childhood into a metaphor for Quebec, and he tells his story against a backdrop of bitter, astute historical analysis. By the end of the book, Vallières' journey through past and present time takes him into the future:

he becomes a member of the revolutionary Front de libération du Québec.

Looking back, *White Niggers of America* was a failure as a revolutionary tract, but while the proletarian uprising Vallières advocated fizzled out in aimless violence, a more bourgeois movement towards Quebec independence has grown into a force so powerful it dominates Canada's political agenda. In *Lament for a Nation*, George Grant had the satisfaction of changing the way people think, but Pierre Vallières enjoyed a writer's greatest triumph – he changed the way we act.

FURTHER READING

Simone de Beauvoir, *The Second Sex*, Vintage Books, 1974. First published in France in 1949, in North America in 1953. My paperback copy describes it as "the classic manifesto of the liberated woman." It is.

Eldridge Cleaver, *Soul on Ice*, Dell, 1968. The black, male American counterpart to *The Second Sex*. Cleaver's use of ghetto slang was as revolutionary in the history of American literature as de Beauvoir's feminist analysis was in French and English. Cleaver's influence can be seen in the work of Tom Wolfe and all the wanna-be-hip American journalists of the 1970s.

Herschel Hardin, *A Nation Unaware*, Douglas & McIntyre, 1974. A fine illustration of how a polemic needs to be well-reasoned and well-documented.

Michael Harris, *Unholy Orders*, Viking/Penguin, 1990. A true crime story freighted with religion and sex. Harris is masterful at translating courtroom testimony into real-life scenarios. *Unholy Orders* is best known in its film version, *The Boys of St. Vincent.*

John A. Livingston, *Rogue Primate*, Key Porter Books, 1994. An environmental sermon in the tradition of Donne and Swift. Livingston integrates scientific language into common English usage.

Kirk Makin, *Redrum the Innocent*, Viking/Penguin, 1992. A superb story about a convicted murderer who, partly because of Makin's book, was proven to be innocent.

Linda McQuaig, *Shooting the Hippo*, Viking/Penguin, 1995. McQuaig is very good at cameo scenes that set up her adversaries as clay pigeons in a shooting gallery. *Kapow! Kapow!* McQuaig is not a writer to lunch with lightly.

Nick Pron, *Lethal Marriage*, Seal, 1995. A thoughtful, objective book about the Bernardo/Homolka murder case by an experienced newspaper reporter. Pron was verbally abused by victims' supporters and his family threatened with violence by a rival writer.

Maggie Siggins, *Revenge of the Land*, McClelland & Stewart, 1991. This saga of Saskatchewan history has everything – true crime, biography, social history, documentary. Maybe it doesn't all belong in one book, but it works!

Walter Stewart, *Shrug: Trudeau in Power*, New Press, 1971. A scathing critique told in Stewart's distinctive peppery voice. Stewart preserves a period of time in the clear amber of his prose.

Larry Zolf, *Dance of the Dialectic*, Lorimer, 1973. What is it about Trudeau that inspired writers? Zolf's satirical analysis is only 112 pages long, but it is as true today as when it was published. Zolf also takes a hilarious run at "Radical Chicci."

CHAPTER 9

Reading Photographs

Photo history has become enormously popular in the past twenty-five years. Public archives have amassed enormous collections of early black-and-white photographs, many of them of superb technical quality, and methods of reproduction are constantly improving. Copyright has lapsed on many of these old photos, or the photographer is unknown, so apart from the cost of reproduction, copies are relatively inexpensive to acquire. Colour reproduction of photographs and paintings, however, has become so expensive that the weighty coffeetable book, once a standard Christmas gift, has gone the way of the dodo. It also fell out of fashion because the thin story content often didn't justify the book's size or price. Any old picture is *not* worth a thousand words; worth depends on the content and quality of the picture, and how it is used.

Choosing photographs for my books is the part of my research I enjoy the most, although in making the final selection I have to balance the quality of the image against the job it will have to do. A picture published in a book is not the same as a picture hanging on a wall or pasted in an album. It is a different size, for one thing. It may be enlarged, or drastically reduced. Enlarging exaggerates a photo's defects – overexposure, spots, blurred focus – yet if it is too small, it may be impossible to decipher the photo's contents.

Discard images with glaring technical defects; a bad picture is worse than none. Readers, I have discovered, read pictures: they expect information from them that complements or enhances the text. They tolerate poor reproduction if the photograph is eloquent, but are easily bored by images, however beautiful, that have no story or context.

A book full of black-and-white pictures, uninterrupted by anecdote or explanation, is static and one-dimensional, yet photos shouldn't be slapped into a text simply for the sake of breaking up a lump of type. Pictures invite readers to pause and rest, words hurry us along; the two have to be orchestrated to work in harmony.

Family snapshots are often worthless. The subjects usually strike poses and put on their best faces, and the amateur photographer may have little concept of lighting or composition. Faces may be in shadow, or turned away, and a picture of tiny figures grouped on a lawn is boring to everyone except the people in it.

Fortunately, most early photographs were taken with good equipment by local professionals, some of them very talented, and their role as chroniclers of community life was later taken over by the ubiquitous press photographer. Many newspapers, especially those that go out of business, donate their morgues to local archives, and these prints and negatives can be a wonderful resource – I recently found some excellent 1937 *Globe and Mail* photos in the City of Toronto Archives. Archives also acquire the holdings of freelance photographers and commercial studios. Keep in mind too that governments and corporations employ photographers to make records of important events, the construction of a subway, for instance, or the introduction of a new product. Who knows what you'll find?

In choosing photos, apply the same basic rules that you do to a story. What is *happening* in this picture? Does it reveal character?

Look for facial expression, strong body language, a background that adds detail and nuance to the subject. Does the photo have social or historical resonance? Is the image well crafted and composed? Finally, how do you feel about this picture? Does it make you sit up and look? Laugh? Hit you in the gut? Does it tell you something you wouldn't have learned anywhere else? Does it express what you are saying better than you could write it yourself?

Finally, identify to the best of your ability the location of the photograph, the year it was taken, and the people or objects in it. "No name" pictures are as exasperating as "no name" stories. Photographs of the same scene taken a year or two apart can show dramatic differences in architecture, landscape, and fashion.

FURTHER READING

J. M. Bumsted, *The Winnipeg General Strike: An Illustrated History*, Watson & Dwyer, 1994. This is an excellent recent example of how fresh, vivid photographs creatively integrated into a text can make a book both easy to read and visually exciting. Also by Bumsted: *The Manitoba Flood of 1950*, Watson & Dwyer.

Edward Cavell, *Journeys to the Far West*, Lorimer, 1979, and *Sometimes a Great Nation: A Photo Album of Canada, 1850-1925*, Altitude, 1984. Two of my favourite books. Cavell, a curator of photography, has an unerring eye, and the quality of reproduction in *Sometimes a Great Nation* makes it a work of art.

Michael Lesy, *Wisconsin Death Trip*, Pantheon, 1973. A stunning collection of photos of frontier Wisconsin orchestrated with fragments of contemporary newspaper stories. One of the first photo histories, this book set the model for many of those that followed.

Susan Sontag, *On Photography*, Farrar, Straus and Giroux, 1973. A thoughtful and provocative essay on the social role of the photograph.

John Szarkowski, *Looking at Photographs*. Museum of Modern Art, New York, 1973. Essential reading. Szarkowski's one-page essay about each picture is as illuminating as the photo itself.

CHAPTER 10

Libel, Copyright, and Other Legalities

The law of libel, or defamation, is so scary writers don't even want to think about it. Ignorance, however, can get us into deep trouble, or intimidate us into needlessly censoring our work.

Libel laws vary from country to country, and, in Canada, from province to province. Many libel suits never progress beyond a threatening letter, and most are settled out of court, on terms that remain strictly secret. Nobody knows how many libel suits are filed every year, who is sued by whom, how many plaintiffs succeed in collecting damages, or how big those damages are.

How do we know what is defamatory? In Canada, the generally accepted legal definition of libel is this: "A defamatory statement is a statement which tends to lower a person in the estimation of right-thinking members of society generally, or to cause him to be shunned and avoided, or to expose him to hatred, contempt or ridicule, or to convey an imputation on him disparaging or injurious to him in his office, profession, calling, trade or business." (Women can be defamed too.)

This leaves a lot of room for interpretation. Plaintiffs don't have to prove they have suffered any actual damage, and the opinions of right-thinking people, whoever they may be, evolve over time and change from place to place. When libel suits go to court, judges and juries express our collective social values in their decisions. They may be liberal or conservative, punitive or generous, fair-minded or bigoted. Damages can range from one dollar to, in a recent Ontario case, $1.8 million.

The law measures reputations in dollars and cents. The most drastic punishment for libel isn't prison, it's bankruptcy. The law also presumes that the person who has published the offending words is guilty. Defendants have to prove the innocence of their words.

If this sounds medieval, it is. The law of defamation was invented as a way of settling questions of personal honour without resorting to fistfights or duels. The best way to deal with a vengeful law is to avoid it.

How? The law offers no safe havens, but libel lawyers have developed reliable guidelines based on generations of judicial decisions. Two Toronto experts, Robert S. Bruser and Brian MacLeod Rogers, include a short, clearly written chapter on defamation in their guidebook, *Journalists and the Law*, published by the Canadian Bar Foundation, 1985. Here are the main things they suggest to keep in mind:

1. You cannot libel the dead, except in Quebec, which operates under the Napoleonic Code. According to British common law, the dead are past suffering damage to their social status or future prospects. Drag all the skeletons you want out of a grave as long as you don't, by association, defame an individual still living.

Never assume someone is dead. Several years ago, I identified a woman involved in an illicit love affair. Her lover had been dead for generations, and although she was much younger than he, I calculated that if she was still living, she would have to be close to one hundred years old. Well, she was! And she didn't complain!

Children and grandchildren can be touchy. They may have a romanticized view of their ancestors, or a keen personal interest in preserving the family reputation. I have received furious letters from elderly great-grandchildren defending the conduct of men who died before they were born. Relatives and friends can't sue for libel unless you specifically implicate them in criminal or abhorrent conduct. If they could, very little history or biography would be written.

2. "I'm telling the truth!" is an airtight defence, if you can prove your statements true in court. We all believe we are writing the truth, but much of our knowledge comes from hearsay, imagination, and wishful thinking. It's no defence to say, "My mother told me," or "I read it in the newspaper." They might be wrong. Accusing someone of a crime, or immoral and unprofessional conduct, is defamatory unless you have witnesses and documents to back you up. Your research must be meticulous and reliable. You can still lose.

3. A class or a group cannot be defamed. This principle was recently reinforced in the Ontario court by Mr. Justice Robert Montgomery. Montgomery dismissed a defamation suit brought by a group of veterans of the Royal Canadian Air Force against the writers and producers of a CBC documentary television series, "The Valour and the Horror." One of the documentary programs depicted the RCAF crews as unwitting participants in the cold-blooded bombing of civilian targets in Germany during the Second World War. The plaintiffs felt they had been depicted as war criminals.

Montgomery found nothing defamatory about the RCAF in the program. He praised the men for their bravery. The only villain, British officer Arthur "Bomber" Harris, had been dead for years, and none of the men bringing the suit had been identified with Harris, or mentioned by name in the program.

Individuals don't have to be named to be defamed. They only have to be recognizable. If a group is small, members can be identified even if no names are used, and using a false name is no help if everyone for miles around knows that "Virginia Gorp" is really Betty Burp. For example, you can castigate school teachers as abusive and incompetent, but not a particular teacher at a specific school. Parents have been sued for statements made in letters they circulated complaining of a teacher's conduct.

Canadian law makes no distinction between individuals and "public figures." Just because people are elected or appointed to public office does not make them fair game for personal criticism, even though we're paying their salaries. In fact, some public figures argue that because of their exposure, they should have greater protection from defamation.

Don't be misled by the House of Commons "Question Period" on television. Members of Parliament and provincial legislatures can say all kinds of cruel and slanderous things about each other within the confines of the chamber, although the Speaker will chastise them for "unparliamentary language." This privilege, however, does not extend to members of municipal councils, school boards, other public agencies, or private citizens.

The law does, however, provide for "fair and accurate" reporting of court proceedings and public meetings, including meetings of administrative boards and committees, commissions of inquiry and their published reports. You can, therefore, quote what these people have said, as long as you do not distort their remarks and refrain from passing judgement or expressing personal biases. Trials, inquiries, and inquests are rich sources of raw material for true stories.

A corporation is considered an individual. Corporations are notoriously touchy about criticism of any kind, especially criticism of their financial performance or business practices. Charities, hospitals, and other non-profit agencies are corporations. So are cities, school boards, and townships. The fact that these corporations are accountable to their shareholders or donors, or to taxpayers, doesn't give the public the right to publish statements the corporations consider to be defamatory.

4. "Don't I have a right to express my opinion?" Yes, you do. Sort of. "Fair comment" is a common defence in libel actions. Fair comment has to be an opinion, not a statement of fact. It can be exaggerated and pig-headed, but it has to be honestly held, based on facts, and concern a matter of "public interest."

Public interest tends to be broadly defined, and we have a great deal of freedom to criticize books and paintings, plays, movies, television shows, concerts, restaurants, and consumer products. The trick is to criticize the book, not the writer, castigate the performance, not the performer. You can write: "Joe Shlunk's book is racist," but not, "This book proves Joe Shlunk is a racist." You can say: "The soup tasted like greasy dishwater," but not, unless you can prove it, "the soup was greasy dishwater." We can condemn the city's lousy garbage collection, but not write, "The mayor and councillors are filthy swine." Cartoonists and satirical publications are able to push the limits because they are not supposed to be taken seriously, but they still get sued.

I was sued over a column I thought was fair comment; the subject disagreed. The problem is: What is fair? People who are publicly criticized, however justly, suffer embarrassment and mortification. They may accuse a writer of "malicious intent" or "false innuendo," and read all kinds of meanings and emotions into a sentence or a phrase. They may demand to see your notes and earlier drafts of your manuscript. They may ask your friends and colleagues if you have ever expressed animosity towards them or an intent to "get" them.

Having a libel lawyer read your manuscript before publication may save you grief, but a legal opinion is simply that, an opinion. (My lawyer thought my column was fair comment too!) Your first precaution is to be absolutely certain of the accuracy of your information and quotations. Major magazines employ professional fact checkers to catch errors in their writers' manuscripts, and it's astonishing how many mistakes they find. Small magazines and book publishers usually don't bother: it's up to you.

Words and phrases can be used in ways that allow the reader to get your point, without giving grounds for litigation. I find that describing people as "intelligent" places them in a benevolent frame of mind, regardless of other things I may say about them. Are they going to sue to prove they're really stupid?

If you have a strong case, chances are good you can beat the plaintiff off with a lawyer's "get lost" letter. People calm down. Once they scream "I'm gonna sue that son-of-a-bitch!" they have proclaimed their innocence. Going through the motions of a suit is a way of saving face, and many libel actions languish and die without being prosecuted. In my case, it was a stand-off. After a public outcry, the plaintiff withdrew his suit against me, and the newspaper that published my column apologized.

Only the rich can afford to have reputations. Libel suits tend to drag on for years, and costs may run into hundreds of thousands of dollars. For writers and publishers, the cost of defending a suit, whatever its merits, can be catastrophic. Libel suits are often trivial and meretricious, but the law provides no quick, clear way of separating these cases from legitimate claims. Publishers prefer to apologize, with or without the writer's consent, and, if necessary, pay an out-of-court settlement. These hypocritical apologies can be humiliating for the writer, but readers tend to accept them for what they're worth, and ignore them. In extreme cases, a frightened publisher will recall a book or magazine from the stores and pulp it.

As far as I'm concerned, the libel law is perverse. A law intended to afford private citizens some protection against public vilification is now used by public corporations to shroud their activities from the legitimate scrutiny of private citizens. Powerful individuals sue, or threaten to sue, to keep out of the public eye. Repeating a defamatory statement, or even writing about it, may embroil other writers and publications in the law suit. If stories about a controversial person or company suddenly vanish from the media, you can bet that somebody has been sued.

Without accurate information about these people or their activities, how can we make the right decisions? Ignorance makes us vulnerable to propaganda, manipulation, and exploitation. We may live in an Age of Information, but how much of it is concealed? Ten per cent? Fifty? Ninety? How will we ever know?

Writers and lawyers have tried for years to persuade governments and the courts that the laws of defamation violate Canada's Charter of Rights and Freedoms. No progress has been made, perhaps because politicians and judges tend to be sensitive about their own reputations. In Great Britain, however, the House of Lords recently ruled that government bodies cannot sue for libel. It is a promising precedent. In the United States, writers can make false and defamatory statements about "public figures" as long as they honestly believe these statements to be true and have diligently attempted to uncover the facts.

I think Canadians tend to err on the side of timidity. Writers and publishers are too easily frightened into thinking that *all* criticism is defamatory. We put up with too much secrecy and intimidation, tolerate too much puffery. This is a democracy, after all, and we do have a right to point out mistakes and misconduct. The more serious the problems, the greater our obligation to publicize them. Be brave. Write what you believe to be true and important and worry about it before you publish it. Most major publishers carry libel insurance and routinely have stories or manuscripts "lawyered." Some writers and publishers take the precaution of checking potentially litigious material with the people implicated. They may be angry, but suing for libel could hold them up to greater ridicule and contempt, as well as allow the defendant's lawyers to probe into potentially embarrassing aspects of their conduct and character. Oscar Wilde's life was destroyed by a libel suit, and he was the plaintiff.

INVASION OF PRIVACY

Can someone sue you simply because you have written about them without their permission? Almost never. Canada's privacy laws are intended to prevent governments, companies, or other institutions, such as schools and hospitals, from publicizing financial, medical, or other sensitive information about private citizens.

This information can, however, be entered as evidence at public trials and inquiries. Writers may come into possession of "restricted" documents. If the documents are authentic, and the information true, they can be freely published.

Only five Canadian provinces have invasion of privacy laws: British Columbia, Saskatchewan, Manitoba, Quebec, and Newfoundland. Quebec's law is the most restrictive: people are entitled to privacy unless they are participating in a public event. Privacy laws, however, are intended to deal with very serious problems: stalking, harassment, spying, and electronic monitoring. Invasion of privacy suits are very rare.

Don't worry about concealing identities or asking people to sign waivers. Canadians have thicker skins, and a stronger appreciation of freedom of expression, than we give ourselves credit for. Early in my career, I was assured by the *Toronto Star*'s fearless theatre critic, Nathan Cohen: "All publicity is good publicity." I often repeat Cohen's adage to myself in stormy weather. The Duke of Wellington had the right attitude. When the Iron Duke's mistress threatened to publish her diaries and his love letters, Wellington replied: "Publish, and be damned!"

COPYRIGHT AND PLAGIARISM

The Duke's mistress had the right to publish her diaries, but not his letters. A letter, journal, manuscript, or other document, published or unpublished, is the property of the writer, unless the copyright has been assigned, in writing, to someone else. Copyright does not have to be registered. Just be sure to put your name on your manuscript.

Your manuscript is your "intellectual property." It is very difficult, however, to copyright ideas, opinions, or experiences which are intangible, highly publicized, or likely to be shared by others. You cannot copyright your life story, only your written autobiography. People involved in sensational public events cannot use copyright to keep others from writing about them. Their story enters the "public domain."

If you appropriate another writer's work as your own, word for word, without acknowledgement, you have committed plagiarism. Students are the worst culprits, but a lot of hack writers blatantly "crib" from other sources. If you use only a few words, or a sentence or two, you will probably get the benefit of the doubt. Plagiarism can be unintentional, and an aggrieved writer is usually satisfied with an apology. Wilfully plagiarizing whole paragraphs or chapters, however, often costs writers their careers and reputations.

If you want to use passages from other books, magazines, or documents, identify them with quotation marks and acknowledge the author and title in your text or in the notes. Few authors object to their work being quoted, but you have to get permission from them or their publishers. If the work is out of print, the writer will often give permission for free, or in exchange for a copy of your book. In my experience, copyright permission fees rarely run higher than two hundred dollars for substantial excerpts. No permission is needed if the writer has been dead for more than fifty years.

If the publisher has gone out of business, and you have no idea how to contact the writer, contact national writers' and publishers' organizations. The company may have been absorbed into a larger firm, or the author may have died. When all fails, go ahead. If an outraged author suddenly surfaces, it is usually sufficient to offer an explanation and a standard fee.

Libraries, archives, and museums normally require only to be acknowledged as the source of the documents you have quoted. Archival material tends to be in the public domain, and archives try to acquire copyright from donors. If they do not have copyright, they should be able to direct you where to get permission.

Photographs and illustrations are also intellectual property and cannot be reproduced without permission unless they have been freely circulated to the media. Expect to pay a fee of ten to thirty dollars to have a photo copied, and up to one thousand dollars for the right to reproduce it. The price can be stiff because "visuals" are in big demand by advertisers and television producers. Old photos and family snapshots, however, may be obtained virtually free.

Beware of publishers who expropriate your copyright, or who pressure you to assign your copyright to them for free or for a token compensation. DO NOT DO THIS. Intellectual property is the Eldorado of the electronic economy. In a corporate stampede to grab anything, everything, much of it may be sand, but who, in the long run, can predict that my shortest story, or your humblest book, will not be worth a fortune?

Hang on, unless you decide to donate or bequeath your copyright to a library, archive, or other public institution. This will qualify you for a tax deduction, but you can still get a deduction for donating your papers without surrendering copyright. On the other hand, archives are so stressed for space they may be forced to reject significant collections. If you care what happens to your own published books, unpublished manuscripts, and other memorabilia after your death, and if you feel your children have other things on their minds (they do), then find out what sort of material archives will accept. I have chosen the University of Manitoba Archives, but they don't have my copyright.

HATE LITERATURE

It is a crime in Canada publicly to advocate genocide, or wilfully to incite hatred likely to lead to violence, against identifiable groups distinguished by colour, race, religion, ethnic origin, or sexual orientation. (Hatred directed towards individuals would be considered defamatory.) Given the multiplicity of groups, and the militancy of many of them, writers who tread on sensitive racial or religious toes are often accused of publishing hate literature. This is almost never true.

The law defends our right to publish true statements and to argue in good faith about religion. We can also publish statements we believe, on reasonable grounds, to be true on subjects of public interest, and can cite examples of genocide or hatred in order to condemn them.

Several years ago, a number of Canadian writers representing racial minorities complained about "appropriation of voice." They particularly resented white writers expropriating aboriginal legends, or writing satirical fictional stories about real native communities. Accusations of censorship and racism were flung about on both sides, then all the writers went back to writing about whatever they wanted to write about.

Culture clash can provide very rich story material, but if you cross cultural or community boundaries, and say uncomfortable things about what you find there, be prepared for controversy. Remember, controversy sells books!

OBSCENITY

Pornography is usually considered fantasy or fiction – the Marquis de Sade may be an exception – and public attitudes tend to be tolerant unless the stories involve extreme violence or sex with children. Publishing sexually explicit *true* stories, however, is a riskier business. Women can write fairly freely about enjoying rough sex (we're supposed to) and lesbian memoirs have had an underground chic for more than a century. There is a whole confessional literature written by survivors of incest and sexual abuse, but a male adult who writes about performing acts depicted in pornography faces prosecution or social ostracism, especially if he's homosexual, and enjoys it.

Many years ago, Toronto writer Gerald Hannon published an article, "Men Loving Boys Loving Men," in a gay newspaper. Hannon interviewed several unidentified men who saw nothing wrong with having sex with underage boys. It was provocative reporting, but it was not obscene, and Hannon went on to a successful career as a freelance journalist. Long after the uproar had been forgotten, however, the story was resurrected as part of an anti-pornography campaign that eventually forced Hannon, a gay activist, out of his teaching job at Ryerson Polytechnic University.

Publishers are not keen to print stories that invite obscenity charges or confiscation of their books and magazines by police. Gay and lesbian bookstores have been routinely raided, their stock seized and shipments of books held up for inspection at customs. Public libraries and mainstream bookstores shy away from publications that upset their more conservative patrons. In Ontario, libraries and booksellers in several communities have refused to stock books about particularly vicious murders, even though the books, by professional journalists, were well-written, accurate, and based on courtroom testimony.

Police are especially vigilant when it comes to sexually explicit publications involving children, and publication includes material distributed on the Internet. Maximum sentence for possessing such material is five years in prison, for making it, ten years. Threat of prosecution makes it difficult to write about taboo subjects, and the defence of "artistic merit" tends to be limited to fiction.

CHAPTER 11

Romancing a Publisher

Publishing your story may turn out to be the easiest part of your writing adventure, especially if you are prepared to publish it yourself. You can experiment with publishing on the Internet. Some book writers, for instance, have created a demand for their work by offering sample chapters, free, to Net surfers; to get the rest of the story, the surfers have to order the book by e-mail or go to a bookstore. Magazines are also marketed this way, and the Web, with its immense potential market, is becoming more attractive to advertisers.

Still, it costs money to get up on the Net, and time, as well as money, to set up and monitor your own home page. Web sites have to be designed, then regularly updated and redesigned. If you don't have much product to promote, and you and your family are not technofreaks, the effort and cost of doing this is prohibitive.

If, like me, you still love the *feel* of a book or a magazine, and you'd rather be writing, advances in computer programs and printing, and the relatively low cost of photocopying, have made self-publishing an attractive option. It is ideally suited to family historians and other writers whose target audience is small, or who do not intend to sell their work. For the rest of us, however, self-publishing should be a last resort. I'll deal with the pros and cons later in this chapter.

The best way to break into print is to sell a story, a column, an editorial, or an excerpt from the book you are writing to a newspaper or magazine. Forget the literary magazines. They don't consider true stories to be literature, and will at best ghettoize your work as "life writing" or "creative non-fiction." They rarely pay, and their readers are few.

Mass-market, mainstream magazines are tough to crack because they rely on pools of professional freelancers who can write quickly to deadline and know what the editors want. Women's magazines, however, are often on the lookout for dramatic, it-happened-to-me stories about trendy issues and these contributors occasionally go on to professional careers. Barbara Frum, for instance, got her start by writing short articles on domestic subjects for the Toronto press. Newspapers such as the *Globe and Mail* regularly publish contributions from the public. A strong letter to the editor might lead to a career as a pundit.

Try the local weekly paper, or, if you belong to a cultural minority or special interest group, a newspaper that targets this market. Check out all the small, specialty magazines in your field of interest. Look for those that suit your style, and try to picture your story published in these magazines. If you find one or two magazines that seem promising, buy them and *read* them. The single biggest mistake writers make is submitting stories or proposals to editors whose publications they have never read. Don't expect a small alternative magazine to pay well. Some do, most don't.

Submit to one publication at a time. Find the editor's name on the masthead. Write this person a covering letter, enclosing your story, or fax a query letter asking if they might be interested in your topic. Indicate that you are familiar with the magazine. Your letter should be well-written and to the point. Do not use garish paper, bizarre type, or a hard sell. Your manuscript should be neatly printed, double-spaced, on white paper, with margins wide enough to scribble in, but not so wide your story looks like a poem. If you hear nothing after two weeks, follow up with a phone call. Personal contact may get things rolling, or confirm rejection. If you leave two messages and get no reply, assume your story has been rejected. Do not call again, but try later with another idea. If you strike out three times, go elsewhere.

Can an editor steal my story idea?

Essentially, yes. A publication can't print your story verbatim, or use quotes from it, without permission, but it may reject your manuscript, then assign the idea, or a similar one, to another writer. Editors ritually deny doing this, but it happens all the time. It's infuriating, but story ideas can't be copyrighted. If you pitch an editor on the phone, make notes of the conversation. If your proposal is rejected, and the same publication runs an identical story six months later, you have evidence to take to the grievance committee of your local writers' organization. It may not get you far, but it might stop the publication doing it to someone else. Your best protection is to put a unique spin or slant on your story that can't be duplicated by another writer.

Be wary of editors who stall, or who praise your story with vague promises of future publication. A story should be accepted or assigned *in writing* within four weeks. Many editors like verbal agreements, but these leave writers vulnerable if editors disappear or change their minds. If no letter is forthcoming, fax the editor a note stating your terms. Set a deadline for a reply, after which you will submit the story elsewhere. Negotiate your fee, and note whether it is paid on acceptance or on publication – publication could be years down the road. The contract should also specify the delivery date, the theme and length of the story – you don't want it cut to shreds – and give you the right to approve the edited version before publication.

Do not write for free unless you are contributing to a charitable cause. When I was starting out, I was told: "We can't pay you, but you'll get your name in the paper!" I didn't buy that, and I got paid. Everybody else in publishing gets paid, why not writers? Our fees are low enough as it is. In Canada, the standard rate for a major magazine story has been one dollar a word for twenty years; many publications, especially newspapers, pay much less. It's gross and hateful, but freelance writers have very few bargaining rights.

If you are a newcomer, expect rock-bottom rates. If, after more than one published story, your fee is still ridiculously low, or you suspect another writer is being paid more for similar work, ask for a raise. At the same time, don't inflate the value of your work to the point where no one will buy it, or behave as if you've won the Nobel Prize. If you feel you are being treated unfairly, contact the Periodical Writers Association of Canada or the Writers' Union of Canada. They will be able to tell you something about the publisher's habits and reputation, and you may find you are not alone. They will also advise you on how to bargain for a higher fee, and may be able to direct you to a better market for your work. Never be timid about asking for money. If you don't value your own work, no one else will.

Your magazine story may bring you to the attention of a book publisher, but if you're not this lucky, a record of periodical publication will give you credibility when you try to sell a manuscript or a book proposal. Remember, yours is only one of hundreds of unsolicited proposals and manuscripts publishers receive every year, and almost all are rejected.

It's always a good idea to sell a book you haven't written yet. Your proposal tests the publisher's interest, and saves you wasting time writing a book nobody wants. But if you are unknown and unpublished, your chances are slim, and your "sale" may be nothing more than a letter from an editor wishing you well. However, if you are able to get a research grant, a publisher may be more willing to offer a contract and an advance against future royalties.

Does it help to have an agent? Yes, but if you are not a celebrity or a professional writer, and this is your first book, you will have difficulty persuading an agent to represent you. Ask yourself: Is my book going to sell enough copies to be worth an agent's time and effort? Is it worth my while to pay an agent fifteen per cent of my royalties? How well can I sell it myself?

The best time to call an agent is when you are offered a contract. How do you get the contract? Do some research. Take a look at *The Canadian Writers' Market* (McClelland & Stewart) and ask your librarian to show you recent publishers' catalogues. Look for the companies that market books like yours. You may discover publishers you've never heard of, including one that specializes in your genre. Search the bookstores and note publishers of books similar to yours. Be realistic. Is your book suitable for a major national or international company, or will it stand a better chance with a local or regional firm? Your goal is not fame or wealth. Your goal is to get published.

Target one or two firms. Get the name of the editor, or of an editor who handles non-fiction. If it's a small, local enterprise, you may be able to talk about your book on the phone or meet the editor in person. Otherwise, write the editor a letter. Enclose a brief outline of your book and one or two sample chapters. Editors are more likely to glance through a handful of pages than tackle a manuscript that looks like a concrete block. If you want your submission returned, send a stamped, self-addressed envelope. It's acceptable to send your work to more than one book publisher at a time, but tell them in your letter that you are doing this.

Wait at least a month before phoning. The editor may have been too busy to look at your manuscript, or may have sent it to outside readers for appraisal. Don't pester, scream, swear, or invite the editor to lunch. On the other hand, don't accept a lot of blah, blah, blah. One publisher sat on my manuscript for a year, putting me off with assurances that an editor was hard at work on it and my contract would soon be in the mail. When I eventually signed with another company, he returned my manuscript immediately, untouched.

An agent will get you a better contract, but you can also get dependable free advice from the writers' organizations. They assist writers who do not qualify to be members, and they may be able to plug you into a capable lawyer who will negotiate your contract for a one-time fixed fee. Most lawyers know nothing about publishers' contracts.

These contracts are horrible. No two are the same, and they take advantage of writers so thrilled with the idea of being published we'll sign anything. Hang on to all or most of the secondary rights, especially film, television, and electronic. Your book probably won't make millions, but you never know when Hollywood might come calling. A standard royalty is calculated as a percentage of the retail selling price of the book. The writer's basic cut is ten per cent, but this will likely be less if the book is printed in paperback, or sold to book clubs and other agencies. Your royalty percentage may increase according to the number of copies sold. Don't accept a contract that offers you a share of the profits: by the time the publisher deducts expenses, you could be left with nothing. And make sure copyright is in your name.

Money is one of those things most writers hate to think about, but money seals a contract. An advance against royalties, whether one thousand dollars or one million, persuades a publisher to invest enough money in your book to earn it back. Publishers who do not pay advances have no money, or no confidence in your book. Remember, an advance is not a gift from the publisher, it's *your* money and will be deducted from your earnings. However, if your book fails to earn enough to cover your advance, you won't be expected to return it. You are obliged to return the advance if you fail to complete the book, or withdraw your manuscript.

Once your manuscript is accepted, don't expect it be published as is. You will likely have to cut, reorganize and rewrite, or let an editor do it for you. Some writers welcome this opportunity to groom and polish, others resent messing around with something they feel is the best they can do. Remember, your editor is your first objective reader. If you look at your story from the editor's point of view, you will notice all kinds of things wrong with it. Fix them, but object to changes you believe trivialize or distort your story. You have the last word. You also have the right to make suggestions (and complaints) with respect to the title, cover, and design. Choosing the title is often the most agonizing part of the whole adventure.

What if all fails? Publishers reject you, your family regards you with pity, the cat won't pee on your manuscript. Is this time for the bottom drawer? The fireplace? Probably. That's why self-publishing has been called the vanity press for so many years. However, if you have faith in your work, producing your own book can be a lot of fun, and some self-published books do become best-sellers.

Look around for a copy shop, a printing house, or a freelance graphic designer who has computer software for desktop publishing. A good copy shop will offer professional design assistance, a wide variety of typefaces and papers, and excellent reproduction of photographs in both black-and-white and colour. You'll probably have to make do with a plastic spiral binding. A printing house will produce any kind of book you want, depending on your financial resources, and as many copies as you require.

Do you intend to sell your book? If so, invest in as professional a product as you can afford. It will appeal more to booksellers, and you can charge more for it. There are many ways to market your book. All it takes is hustle. Deliver a few copies to all the independent bookstores you think might be interested. They may not buy them, but they might display a couple to see how they go. Remember, the bookstore will take forty per cent of the retail price. Approach the buyer for a big superstore chain. They need product, and your book might find a niche. Don't print too many copies – if they end up in the dump, you'll still be stuck with the bill.

Try to place copies in local gift shops and specialty stores. Sell your book at fairs and flea markets, through clubs and newsletters or by mail. Persuade the local newspaper to give you a write-up, and get an interview on cable television. Advertise. If the book arouses interest, you may be able to persuade a publisher or distributor to take over marketing.

Expect to promote your own book whoever publishes it. The fly-by-night, if-this-is-Edmonton-it-must-be-Tuesday publicity tour is usually the last perilous stage on our pilgrim's progress. Most writers aren't used to being interviewed, and you may feel nervous and tongue-tied on radio and television. The trick is to memorize three or four key points about your book, and make sure you blurt them out. Don't ramble. Tell good, short anecdotes from your book, stories that will stick in people's minds, and, most important of all, mention your book's title again, and again, and again. It feels stupid, I know, but if people in the audience remember a single word of it when they get to the bookstore, you'll be in luck. That's why serious books about economics have titles like *Shooting the Hippo* or *Wrestling with the Elephant*. The danger, of course, is that *Shooting the Hippo* could end up on a shelf with animal rights books, and *Wrestling with the Elephant* in sports.

This happens. In my local library, *Shooting the Hippo* is catalogued under Death.

In the excitement and celebration of seeing your story in print, prepare yourself for apathy, criticism, and disappointment. Your book may not be reviewed for months, or some nincompoop will hate it. A hostile review, however, is better than none at all, and if it provokes controversy, better yet. You'll be interviewed by people who haven't opened your book, don't know what it's about, and couldn't care less. You will not find your book in many stores, or you might locate a single scruffy copy in a dark corner. You may be nominated for a prize, and not win, or not be nominated for a prize you feel you deserve. Sales will probably be below expectations. If your phone doesn't ring, and you overhear your publicist calling your book a dog, things are going badly.

It's a humbling experience. I have learned to expect the worst so I can always be pleasantly surprised. I regard my published book as a box of cereal: its success or failure will depend as much on marketing, promotion, timing, and popular taste as on the quality of its contents. By this time I don't really care, I'm hard at work on my next story.

THE CANADIAN WRITER'S MARKET

A COMPREHENSIVE GUIDE FOR FREELANCE WRITERS

JEM BATES
WITH AN INTRODUCTION BY ADRIAN WALLER

Success in getting your manuscript published depends on knowing where you are most likely to sell your work, who to approach and how, and where to find professional and financial assistance.

In the ever-changing and increasingly competitive world of Canadian publishing, this is not as easy as it might sound. The indispensable tool for keeping up is *The Canadian Writer's Market*, acclaimed coast to coast for more than twenty-five years as the most impor-  tant reference book for writers, next to a dictionary and thesaurus. It includes the most comprehensive and up-to-date list- ings available for:

- consumer magazines
- literary and scholarly journals
- trade, business, and professional publications
- daily newspapers
- book publishers.

The Canadian Writer's Market also includes listings for literary agents, awards, competitions, and grants, and offers practical advice on all aspects of manuscript preparation and marketing. It also contains useful background information on the thorny issues of income tax for the freelancer and copyright and libel law.

"This splendid book is the best and least expensive reference available for would-be authors. It contains everything they need to know about how and where to submit a manuscript."
— Laurel Boone, Editorial Director, Goose Lane Editions

A PASSION FOR
NARRATIVE

A GUIDE FOR WRITING FICTION

JACK HODGINS

This book is not intended to persuade you to take up writing novels or short stories – "It's going to be a lot of work," Jack Hodgins warns. Nor will it tell you how to market your stories. But it will take you through the problems facing any fiction writer and show you how some of the best writers in English have solved them.

As an award-winning novelist and short-story writer, Jack Hodgins is uniquely qualified to preach what he practises. As a trained teacher, he has been giving creative writing lessons for more than thirty years, at high schools and universities and to writers' summer schools. In recent years his creative writing courses at the University of Victoria have become discreetly famous. Now, anyone who buys this book can share in the experience of learning fiction-writing from a master.

With its scores of examples of first-class writing, this lively, truly fascinating book will almost certainly make you a better writer; it is guaranteed to make you a better reader.

"One excellent path from original to marketable manuscript.... It would take a beginning writer years to work her way through all the goodies Hodgins offers."
– GLOBE AND MAIL

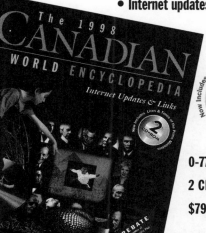

A Short History of CANADA
DESMOND MORTON

"General readers will be pleasantly surprised to find that a professional historian has written a book that is a joy to read, succinct, sensible, and well balanced in its viewpoint as well as in its coverage." – ROBERT BOTHWELL

Most of us know bits and pieces of our history, but would like to be more sure of how it all fits together. The trick is to find a history that is so absorbing you will want to read it from beginning to end. With this new, expanded edition of **A Short History of Canada**, updated to the 1990's, you need look no further. "Had such a book been available a generation ago," says the Montreal *Gazette*, "the canard that Canadian history is dull might never have got off the ground."

In one compact and remarkably comprehensive volume, DESMOND MORTON, called "a first-rate storyteller" by the *Toronto Star*, pulls off the remarkable feat of bringing all of Canadian history together – from Sir John A. Macdonald to Jean Chretien, from Jacques Cartier to Lucien Bouchard.

Trade Paperback • 5¹/4" x 8¹/4" • 352 pages

HOW TO BUY A COMPUTER
Or Upgrade What You Have
MYLES WHITE

"Using simple language and patient explanations, White covers all the bases, and then some… All of his explanations are wonderfully clear, simple, and well-researched." – QUILL & QUIRE

For a writer, the computer has become as indispensable as the pencil and eraser. But buying a new computer or upgrading your existing system can be a daunting experience because of the arcane terminology associated with the technology and the dizzying number of options available in the marketplace.

MYLES WHITE, author of *How to Buy a Computer*, is a computer columnist and feature writer for the *Toronto Star* and a regular contributor of articles to the U.S. magazine *Computer Currents*. He's also associate editor of the plain-English computer newspaper *We Compute*, where he writes a monthly column, special features, and reviews. He regularly conducts seminars on buying and upgrading computers for the Computer Fest shows, and presents a television version of his column, "The White Pages," as part of "Discovery.EXN."

Trade Paperback • 6" x 9" • 252 pages • b&w line drawings